PRAISE FOR *A SPONTANEOUS LIFE*

"During my time filming a show for Netflix in Vancouver, Danny David was my trainer. His ability to listen, empathize, motivate, and focus on the smallest of details is second to none. His story is the apotheosis of true courage and offers us powerful insights on overcoming any obstacle, however challenging and seemingly impossible, so we may live as our best self. And he's shredded."

PATRICK WARBURTON, AWARD-WINNING ACTOR, PRODUCER, AND PHILANTHROPIST

"To know Danny is to be inspired. From his writing and personal training to magazine editorial production, he has always been dedicated to his craft. We've collaborated on many great projects and he has always met every situation with utmost fervor and enthusiasm. He takes what lessons he can at every turn and has always lived his life and followed his dreams so admirably."

LIZ ROSA, PHOTOGRAPHER

"When a person's life starts out with a severe childhood trauma such as a parent leaving at two months old, you have to expect there will be some fallout. When this same person goes through all of life's challenges and ends up being the true champion of his own story, the rest of us should listen. This book is so full of wisdom and gems of inspiration that I'll be recommending it to my clients."
JANEL BALL, M.A., R.C.C., THERAPIST,
TRAUMA AND EMDR SPECIALIST

"For anyone looking to radically improve their life, this book is a must read. Danny shares science-backed, practical, life-changing guidance in such a fun and approachable way with his personal storytelling and experiences. As someone who also helps empower others to make positive changes in their lives, I will be adding this to my resources for my clients."
MANDY KING, HOLISTIC NUTRITIONIST,
FOUNDER OF HEAL WELLNESS

"*A Spontaneous Life* is a captivating read, offering a blend of exceptional storytelling, practical insights, and motivational messages. It's a must-read for anyone seeking to enhance their life through inspiring tales and actionable guidance."
DAI MANUEL, AWARD-WINNING AUTHOR,
LIFESTYLE OPTIMIZATION MENTOR, AND
PERFORMANCE COACH

"I was recovering from pelvic surgery and radiation that forced me into retirement when I started training with Danny. His skills in the areas of building one's confidence, flow of movement, and functional performance has dramatically improved my way of life after cancer treatment. *A Spontaneous Life* is a journey for anyone who is looking forward to the challenges of personal transformation, fostering a positive mindset, and increasing one's quality of life with raw, honest storytelling and a science-based system."
PHILLIP MALPASS, M.D., CANCER CARE PHYSICIAN

"I've known Danny for close to fifteen years. His heart has always been the thing that stuck out to me. It's so open. So caring. So willing to forgive. And so willing to learn. I'm not sure if I've ever met anyone who was as willing to put himself out there. He's faced adversity. He's been to hell and back. But his perseverance, drive, and giant heart kept him going. I am beyond proud of him. His story and the wisdom he shares are well worth your time."
GILES PANTON, ACTOR AND FATHER

"*A Spontaneous Life* is a treasure of wisdom. Truly transformative. I'll recommend it to my clients, knowing that this book is filled with inspiration and insights to spark positive change in someone's life."
ANETTE SKYE ORAN, BUSINESS MENTOR,
PODCASTER, AND COFOUNDER, COHERE.LIVE

"This book is a testament to Danny's extraordinary character. He is a friend who pushes you to be your best, supports you through your lows, and celebrates your highs. His unwavering support over the years has been instrumental in my journey of losing over fifty pounds and allowing me to pursue the active lifestyle I always wanted. I hope his story and insights inspire and resonate with you just as much as they have profoundly impacted my life."
LAURENT BEIQUE, WEB DEVELOPER

"Danny is a man who marches to the beat of his own drum. He is very ambitious, kind to those around him, and truly wants to help change people's lives. I believe his story will encourage many readers to push outside of their comfort zones and change their lives for the better!"
JUDAH RATZLAFF, STRENGTH AND
LIFESTYLE COACH

"I know Danny as a passionate personal trainer and his book captured me immediately. His storytelling around overcoming challenges with valuable lessons learned really resonates with me. This read is captivating and inspiring."
NASTASIA LIAVAS GENOVA, VICE PRESIDENT,
FITNESS SERVICES, FITNESS WORLD CANADA

A SPONTANEOUS LIFE

HOW I MASTERED THE SUBTLE ART OF FLOW

DANNY DAVID

Danny Mind Body
VANCOUVER, CANADA

www.dannymindbody.com

Cover design by Gus Yoo
Editing and book production by Stephanie Gunning

A Spontaneous Life / Danny David —1st edition

ISBN 978-1-7381643-0-1 (paperback)
ISBN 978-1-7381643-1-8 (ebook)

CONTENTS

Spontaneous (adjective): *Developing or occurring without apparent external influence, force, cause, or treatment.*

A Spontaneous Life: Living without hesitation in flow with your instincts, intuition, and intention.

PREFACE

I didn't know what to call it. It was just a gut feeling I had that there was a better way to live. Nothing more. Nothing less. I didn't think much of anything about this inkling. Not at first. Never had I considered that a different way of life was a possibility. Let alone possible for me.

Until I did.

The first thing I will tell you about my discovery is that it changed my life.

This book is proof.

I was a year removed from a devasting bike accident that put me in the back of an ambulance and shook me up. A year back from putting the life I had been living on hold while I recovered. In that year, my life took a major downturn, and I was barely holding things together. My once-thriving, successful personal training business was worth a fraction of what it once was. I had burned through my savings at a terrifying pace, spending tens of thousands of dollars. I couldn't write anymore either—all my years working as a culture and lifestyle journalist seemed almost to vanish overnight. After the accident, I lost my creative discipline.

The absolute worst part of this slump I found myself in was that I couldn't seem to look further ahead than a few days. I felt isolated and uninspired. The past haunted me. Regret had sunk its claws into my shoulders. Any major life goals I had—like the goal of writing a book—seemed to be too far gone, too hard, too impossible even to try.

Making matters worse, I felt out of alignment with my idea of the man I should be. My belief in this guy in my head was wearing me down. I thought I should be stronger. I thought I should be more successful. I thought I should be happier. I thought I should have more friends. I thought I should be a best-selling author. I thought *I should . . . I should . . . I should . . .*

It seemed easier to lay on the couch staring at the wall and thinking about all the things I should be doing than to stand up and eliminate the things I knew were making me unhappy from my life or try to get what I wanted. Every impulse towards action was quickly snuffed.

I had no idea who I was anymore.

Can you relate?

The big difference between my life before the accident and my life after was that my perspective had changed. I wasn't happy anymore. I didn't feel confident. And I wasn't having any kind of real success because I didn't give a crap. But despite my apathy, depression, and stagnation, I did have one thing going for me. Before my accident, I had cared more about what others thought of me than what I thought of myself. Now the opposite was true.

There was also a feeling deep in my gut. A feeling I woke up with every morning. I went to work with it, and it stayed with me in my dreams. A craving.

More than anything, I wanted to change.

I knew I couldn't keep going the way I was. Some way, somehow, I knew change was coming. I felt it everywhere I went. It was like a seed germinating in the soil of my subconscious mind.

Gradually, this feeling I couldn't shake, which didn't even have a name, became something more. My mind went to work diligently deciphering what this possible change would look and feel like. Every day, the picture of my future grew a little bit bigger, a little bit stronger, and a little bit more specific. Every day, it felt more real.

Could I just dismiss all the responsibilities in my current life for a chance at a new one based on this picture? Could I be fearless and spontaneous and take the risk?

The answer in my heart was yes.

Without hesitation.

One day, something just clicked. I stopped thinking about all the things I should be doing and made the decision to become the person I felt I had to be. I committed to my growth. Out of my gut feeling, I generated a vision. In all the mornings and nights spent thinking about change, I had devised a blueprint. I would take a sabbatical off the grid and, in complete solitude, walk a path of healing. I envisioned going someplace remote and peaceful, committing myself to a set of daily rituals that would help me become a better man inside and out—new in body, mind, and spirit. My heart told me the place to go to was Central America.

My spontaneous decision to take a leave of absence from work and go on sabbatical was the beginning of creating an extraordinary new life for myself. When I said yes to this plan of action, I wanted to reconnect with the part of me that knows how to constantly evolve and flow with life and not be stuck on the couch dreaming and always hesitating until it is too late to act.

My plan was to bring myself to the next level in my life by attuning my mind with my authentic being. I hoped to begin living every moment with purpose, not only in spite of my struggles and setbacks but using those struggles as fuel to drive me and mining them for lessons.

What I discovered on that trip was that it is possible to remake yourself. Also, it is near impossible not to find true joy when you are just being the real you. When you're not thinking who you think you should be. When you're being spontaneous. A spontaneous life is a happy life.

The world tests us. Most of us fear our challenges—for whatever reason. Maybe we didn't ask for the test, and it seems unfair. Maybe it's hard, even harder than we expected. Even so, this test that arrives is the essence of our life. Meeting our tests head on gives us the opportunity to master ourselves using remarkable, though often unappreciated and unrecognized skills. How we overcome the circumstances that we believe are impossible to manage defines us.

A lot of life comes down to how we handle fear. By choosing to overcome our fears, we are choosing not to let the past hold us back. By choosing to overcome our fears, we are choosing to live a spontaneous life.

Without fear, none of us would hesitate to take risks to live our best dreams.

This is the message at the center of this book.

In my life, I have faced many challenges. I have learned many lessons and taken my share of risks. In these pages, I will recount some of my stories for you and share my takeaways. The same skills I cultivated and insights I gleaned from the process of achieving success as a champion amateur bodybuilder and elite personal trainer with lifetime sales just south of a million dollars taught me the standards I needed to live by as I investigated what would get me back on track and help me recapture my enthusiasm for living.

My vision was real. But I understood going in that having a vision on its own wasn't going to be enough. My intention was to go deep enough inside my mind and heart to re-engineer my entire belief system. As part of my internal and external reconditioning, I would need to learn to create a peak state at will, a state in which my mind, body, and spirit could connect with my intentions. In part, this book is the story of how I mastered this process.

In this book, I will teach you a simple formula for living into your dreams without fear and hesitation. The first part of the formula involves uncovering your true vision and creating a blueprint for your future built on your authentic desires. The second part involves using spontaneity as a means of constructing that blueprint in the real world, day by day.

Whether you are a leader, a rebel, a free spirit, an artist, or a dreamer—people we think of as being *spontaneous*—or you are someone who maybe thinks of themself as "average" but gets up and does their best as a human being in a conventional nine-to-five job to take care of their family and pay the bills, this way of living without hesitation can change your reality. My intent in sharing aspects of my life story with you is to inspire you to begin putting together the pieces of the beautiful puzzle that is your own spontaneous life.

PART I

LEARNING THE WAYS OF THE WORLD

ONE

WE HAVE THE POWER TO TRANSFORM OURSELVES

Would you like to make a change?

None of us can achieve anything great without enduring many shares of pain and emotional struggle and having bettered ourselves as a result of overcoming obstacles.

Nobody will tell you differently.

We are capable of incredible, seemingly impossible feats of excellence and self-transformation. It happens as a natural result of growth and learning. Every human being has the power to become a better person every day, every minute, every second. This transformation is spontaneous. From the first day of our existence, we transform as we transition from crawling on the ground to walking, and from wordlessly wailing when we need something to speaking. And on and on.

We also have stories we tell ourselves about who we are and that of which we are capable. These inner narratives range from supportive to sinister. Maybe you tell yourself that something you want is impossible. Maybe you believe you can't do it, so "there's no use trying." Although the truth is that you just don't know how to do it yet, it may seem easier to accept this idea than to accept that a major change is going to be needed to get there (wherever *there* is for you).

Your inner narrative may have conditioned you to believe you're too weak or incompetent, and still, in every struggle, no matter how hopeless, there is an idea of the potential that it is possible to be stronger than the struggle. The idea that you could find the avenue to succeed.

As you go to sleep at night and play with the ideas in your mind, do you ever wonder what would happen if you just put in the necessary work and stopped fucking around?

When I was still too young to reach the gas pedals in the car, my father taught me a very important lesson about what we are capable of doing. To be clear, I didn't know my father well because he didn't live with me and my mom, and yet, despite him not being around to teach me all the things a father is supposed to teach his son to make the boy into a man, he did teach me something valuable through his example.

I do not doubt I would have benefitted from seeing him love my mom (thereby showing me how to love women in the same manner), demonstrating leadership skills (allowing me to become more of a leader in my life), teaching me discipline and how to take responsibility and understand consequences, or taking me to baseball games, and so many other things. But he didn't do those things with me.

My dad left my mom when I was two months old. He disappeared for well over a year, leaving her without child support or a phone call. And by "left," I mean he went out of the country. Then one day, as my mom has told me, he just showed up again. "Too little, too late" is how she describes it. We saw each other a handful of times over the next few years. My parents disagreed about custody issues. There were supervised visits with my dad, most times with my maternal grandfather present. Sometimes, I would not see my dad for months, sometimes for years. I never knew why he came when he came or left when he left. Although I had a pretty good childhood, I did miss having a dad who showed up.

I had my share of close friends growing up. But every time I was over at a friend's house for dinner I would see a family that looked like what I thought a family should look like: a father, a mother, an older brother to look up to, a baby sister to bug, a dog, a big house, a big backyard, lots of love, and lots of father-son male bonding—and this made me feel a little empty and a little resentful.

On the surface, I didn't have any disadvantages in my life. I wanted to learn karate, so my mom got me karate lessons, and she was there for every lesson and tournament. She sent me to summer camp for four straight summers and got me piano lessons. (Regrettably, this is not a skill I stuck with.) And when I started falling in love with film and acting, a new world opened up to me. My mom got me a talent agent. Then I started doing small parts on kids' television shows. I pinned movie posters all over the walls of my bedroom. When alone, I imitated scenes from my favorite movies, combining my impressive martial arts training and extremely low splits with Jean-Claude Van Damme's badass roundhouse kicks, and repeating Al Pacino's way-over-the-top dialogue from Tony Montana's classic restaurant scene in *Scarface*: "Say good-bye to the bad guy."[1]

More than once, I played the lead in an elementary school play. The character I most remember playing was a kid being peer-pressured into doing drugs. That performance made me feel more alive than ever before. I recall wishing my dad had come to see the show.

I carried a binder with me everywhere in which I wrote my storylines. These had crazy plot twists and carefully planned endings, plus actions scenes that I would act out. The acting world was wonderful, an escape where I could allow my imagination to be limitless. I was young and believed I could be the world's greatest actor. This was my first taste of feeling spontaneous from moment to moment, and in this newfound world, I felt alive and happy.

One fateful day when I was eleven years old, something happened that immediately moved my life and my relationship with my dad in a new direction. Something I could never have anticipated, whose meaning and magnitude

I did not understand at the time. My mom told me the biggest news I had ever heard: "Danny, your father has cancer."

Just. Like. That.

State of confusion. Overload.

The news was a lot to chew on, especially for a preteen who had just gone to first base for the first time with his girlfriend (that meant putting my tongue in her mouth). Before that event, I'd wanted nothing more than to go home every day after school and watch cartoons.

There are two reasons why I was confused. The first was my limited understanding of what cancer was. Until that moment, the idea of death and dying had never entered my mind—not from being self-aware in thought or from an emotional connection to it. I mean, let's be honest, cancer is not what your average kid thinks about.

Yeah, I know, kind of obvious.

Of course, I'd heard the word *cancer* before but only said in passing or as an afterthought, like hearing someone describe having the flu or being really sick and then getting better. Being a kid who would put his hands on anything I found on the ground, I was sick many times myself. And then I got better.

"Do you know what that means?" my mom asked.

My dad had lung cancer, and it had already spread quite a bit. As best she could, Mom explained the diagnosis to me and what I should prepare myself to see in the coming months and years.

I had seen enough movies at the time in which characters got sick to understand that cancer is one of the worst kinds of sickness; but remember, the movies were my world away from reality, a world that was my own in which I could fully be present. The real world and the movie world were never the same. In the movies and my mind, I was either the superhero or a supercool villain, or perhaps the most popular kid in school stuck in detention with four other misfits and creating havoc on a sunny afternoon. (*Breakfast Club*, anyone?) I could fly like Superman (or Superboy), blow shit up like Arnold Schwarzenegger in *Commando*, and save the girl and the city from destruction. In my movie world, I could have cancer and still give the greatest performance of my life and win an Oscar at a young age. That was the kind of storyline I thought of when I thought of having cancer. I associated it with a golden statue.

My point is that the two worlds were far apart.

The second reason for my confusion? The word *father*. I wasn't quite sure what to make of it, or should I say, I wasn't sure how I was supposed to *feel* about it. What exactly did this word mean? Was I being asked to see this man differently all of a sudden?

I'd always wanted a father. Not a man who came to see me because he felt it was his duty. I felt that the ship had sailed on our relationship because he had never been there when I needed him. And even when he felt compelled to be there, which was rare, I was always in a state of confusion about what I should feel and how I should act—and a little angry.

And I'll tell you, as shocking as the news was to hear that this man who was my biological father had cancer, it wasn't the only shocking news I heard that same day. There was something else my mom told me, something surprising and extraordinary.

"Danny, you have a brother."

My head was spinning. This new news was a lot to handle.

In five minutes, I'd discovered both that my father was fighting for his life and that there was a little kid, only two years old, with the same blood as mine flowing through his veins. The same genetic code had formed every part of his body—meaning, he would probably look almost exactly like me. And I hadn't known that this other family my dad was a part of even existed!

Definitely more revelations than any little kid should ever have to handle at one time.

But I'm not going to lie, hearing the news that I had a kid brother, who himself now had something that I'd never had and would've liked having—an older brother he could look up to and imitate—sparked a little excitement in my soul. He was two and utterly unaware of what was happening and who was who, or that he had an older brother. Would it be strange for him if I just showed up in his life? I immediately thought about how I could be the best older brother ever.

That was all running through the limited catalog of experience in my mind as I was also really trying to feel something about the other news.

For the longest time, I had wanted to hate my dad. For leaving my mom. For leaving me. For depriving me of having the type of family I saw that all my friends had. And now I wanted to hate him for depriving me of a brother I didn't know existed until he got sick. Maybe it was because he was sick. I was so mad that I didn't think he deserved my time or had the right to call me son, or the right to hear me say the words *dad* and *father*. But when my mom told me he had cancer, I also recognized that I had to change the way I felt. Despite my youth, I saw that I couldn't focus on the past and the pain that it brought me. I decided at that moment that anger wasn't going to motivate me anymore.

In retrospect, of course, letting this resentment go took time, but it was something that I decided I wanted to try to do on the same day I got the news. To forgive my dad would require me to wrestle with my anger and sadness and rise above my circumstances.

Before then, my mom had always given me the choice of whether or not to spend time with my father, and let's say that out of a sheer mix of uncomfortableness and fear of saying no to him I saw him at the times I did. It was different this time. She didn't offer me an option. She told me, "You should spend as much time with him as possible, not just because he's your father but because it's the right thing to do. One day, when you're older, you'll understand why."

Of course, I did understand why. I was young enough that I was still figuring out my way in this crazy world, but old enough where I already knew the difference between the right thing to do and the wrong thing to do. Being kind to a sick person was right. Still doing it wasn't as easy as knowing what it was.

Emotions are tricky. My understanding of the reason and my emotional connection to the reason were completely separate. I wasn't capable of full forgiveness yet.

I'll never forget my first trip to the hospital. The occasion was both the first time I saw my dad after hearing that he was sick, and the first time I met my brother. The feeling I had that day was as intense a feeling as I can remember from my childhood, right up there with the thrill of performing my first lead in a school play in front of the entire school and my family, and of course, the first boob I ever touched at summer camp. (The girl's name was Francisca. I was ten or eleven. It was great.) Each one of these experiences had a certain kind of uncomfortableness added, a mixture of fear and excitement. You know.

I remember being in the elevator as the doors to the cancer ward opened, and instantly, the smell was nothing I had ever experienced. Sudden and fast, it hit me like a ton of bricks.

What's this smell? Is this what death smells like? I wondered. I know it sounds harsh, but this is what was going through my mind.

We walked down the hallways and as we passed every room I peeked inside and I saw women and men, young and old, in bed sitting up or standing surrounded by family and loved ones, or all alone. Each person in a robe had tubes sticking out of his or her chest. Seeing this, all of a sudden what I had only seen in movies became very real to me.

We got to my father's room, and a sense of fear washed over my body and mind. I was confused by what I was feeling. I saw my father lying in his hospital bed, wearing the same robe I saw everybody else in the hospital ward wearing, and with the same sorts of tubes plugged into his body.

I clenched my mother's arm for dear life and looked down at my father lying in his hospital bed. When I saw him look right back at me, a chill hit me. I saw a smile on his face that I had never seen on it before. He was so happy to see me. Not like all the other times before then. Maybe I had never been looking closely enough on those other occasions. Maybe I had been just too angry and too uncomfortable to read his face as smiling at me. But now I saw the unmistakable happiness in his eyes and the tears of joy that soon followed.

It was very uncomfortable.

Then I witnessed something else, a phenomenon I'd never seen before. My mom went over to my dad and embraced him. I stood at the door and watched my mom hug this man about whom she'd never had many kind words to say, and it wasn't just a quick hug or a pat on the back. The embrace was meaningful and real, and it lasted maybe ten seconds. She meant it.

And even after the hug, she didn't move away; she still held onto my dad's arms and asked how he was feeling. She meant that too.

I thought I was going to see my dad without hair and skinny and looking as sick as a very sick person could look—like in the movies—but he didn't look like any of that. He looked exactly like the last time I had seen him. It had been at least a year.

He called me over and gave me a massive hug like he was trying to win the Guinness world record for hugs. Then we chatted for a while. Or, he chatted while I listened. I didn't talk much.

Not that I remember where this was, but I do recall that the same day I met an adorable little kid with absolutely no idea what was going on or who I was. Whereas I had thought I was going to meet a mirror image of myself, Jonathan, my baby half-brother, turned out to be far from it. I have brown hair and super dark brown eyes. Jonathan was a little cutie with flowing blond hair and shiny blue eyes, as was his mother, a lady who stood five-nine to my mom's petite five-four. I knew that one day my brother would tower over me. (He's now six-three. I'm five-ten.) But still, he was my brother, and it was pretty damn cool to have a sibling.

Now, everything was as right as rain, right?

Not exactly.

After my father's initial surgery, he was eventually released from the hospital, making frequent return visits for chemotherapy. He had a place not too far from our home and over the next year I saw him, along with my little brother, every two weeks. During that year, I watched my father's condition deteriorate. The chemo took hold of him. Physically, weight was coming off him quickly, and he lost all his hair. His spirits nonetheless remained high. He tried everything to heal, including turning to spirituality. He attended satsang with gurus and had sessions with spiritual healers, trying their alternative therapies. He wanted to live and wasn't giving up. His desire to live wasn't a question.

We all can find ourselves in a place in our lives where things just aren't working for us, times when we think we need an escape. I saw that my father was so much more than his mistakes. When I finally realized that he had so much more to offer, I saw a man who wasn't letting his past define him. I saw a man who knew he could transform.

We each have the power to transform. Most times, we allow our past behaviors, habits, and emotional responses to dictate our current lives. But the truth remains, we each have the power to change the way we think about ourselves, our current situation, and our place in this world. We can look back at our mistakes and use them as lessons to change and transform. We can use our current struggles as a source of strength. This is not only our power. This is our responsibility—for our kids, parents, friends, and anyone who we have affected and have the power to affect. Knowing we can transform and accepting this amazing power with ownership is our human responsibility.

Somehow, as we are facing our mortality, we are given a new choice, an opportunity to transform ourselves and form a different ideology about who we are. My father chose to fight for his life with everything he had. And part of his fight was to make right the wrong he did to me. That meant trying to be a better father to me. Father of the Year. It also meant finding peace within himself by elevating his human spirit.

That's at the core of the lesson he taught me through his example.

Between you and me, he wouldn't be able to erase how I felt about over a decade of neglect no matter what he did. Even so, I could see he was a man seeking redemption. I understood he wanted to connect with me in a new way and given his situation I kept the truth of my inability to entirely forgive him buried inside me so I could give myself over to the relationship.

My father fought his cancer every step of the way and truly believed he could beat it. Every time I visited him, there seemed to be more life in him. Hell, I started to believe he could beat it too. I thought he could until the very end. This belief is the reason why I wasn't prepared for it when the end came. I didn't see it coming.

I had just spent the previous week with him, and he was doing fine. We had watched some movies at his place, and I played with my little brother. I remember that I had brought my schoolbooks with me to study for a math exam I wanted to do well on. I hated math, especially algebra, which was the subject of the exam. My dad tried to help me study, but to be honest, he wasn't any better at it than me. Even so, he made a valiant attempt.

About a week later, I came home after school to complete silence and darkness. Usually, my mom would be home preparing dinner at that time. I had the exam I'd studied for all week in my hand with a big fat 90 percent mark in red ink written by the teacher at the top of the page next to the words *GREAT JOB*, and I was feeling pretty damn good about myself. I posted the paper on the fridge while I waited for somebody to show up. I was one proud fourteen-year-old.

The house phone rang. Finally. It was my mom. I immediately told Mom about my grade, right before she told me where she was. At the hospital. Dad had gone into septic shock and been rushed to the emergency room, still alive. She told me she would come to get me and to hold on tight. About an hour or so passed, then she walked in. I had my shoes and jacket on and was ready to go, but we weren't going anywhere.

Two words were all my mom said. "He's gone."

The moment I was not ready for had come.

I stood there in complete silence.

"He smiled when I told him how well you did on your algebra exam." It was the last thing he heard.

I went to my room that evening. I tried to connect with the feeling of loss. I wanted to find something, anything I could feel, an outlet, a source of pain, something I could release. But there were no tears. I lay on my bed and thought about how he was trying to help me with the exam the previous week and how in his last few moments, which I'm sure he knew would be his last, he'd smiled knowing I had done well. But I couldn't cry for him that night.

The weight of guilt for my inability to mourn my dad weighed heavily on my shoulders. I wanted to be able to cry so much, but it just wasn't coming out. I wanted to feel that it wasn't for nothing—all the hospital visits and overnight stays at his place. Could I, even after everything that had transpired, not move on from where I was two years before?

Was I still angry at him?

The funeral for my dad was massive. He had an enormous family of origin, with eight brothers and sisters, so I met tons of new cousins. It was the first funeral I'd ever attended. My brother was so young and innocent that he didn't know what had happened or why we were there. The entire family and all the guests made our way from the viewing room to the burial site right outside. Tears were flowing everywhere I looked. My uncles and aunts were crying. My cousins were crying. Friends of my dad and friends of friends were crying. And still, I didn't shed a tear.

My baby cousin Sheena, seven at the time, was standing next to me and said something I'll never forget. A question that left me stunned.

"Why are you the only one not crying?"

That bothered me. It hurt me and felt like a deep cut in my heart because it made me question what kind of person I was. I didn't say anything. I didn't respond. I kept to myself for the remainder of that day and chose to keep my feelings to myself. Instead of allowing myself to feel what I was genuinely feeling, I questioned why I wasn't feeling something else. I knew nobody understood what I was going through;

they seemed to expect me to grieve like everybody else was grieving. But I couldn't grieve openly, as much as I tried.

I mourned the death of my dad without shedding a tear because I couldn't separate the man who had left me from the man who had fought to live and find my forgiveness. Of course, I was a child, so those types of distinctions were beyond me. But as an adult, I see him differently.

My father wasn't there for my karate lessons and school plays. He didn't show me how to throw a football, take me to baseball games, or give me the awkward birds-and-bees speech. He wasn't a husband to my mom. I choose not to stay fixated on sad moments and to remember that in his darkest hours, Dad found enlightenment. He discovered his human spirit and will to live. He did not give up when he faced death.

In dying as he did, my dad demonstrated that each of us has the choice until the end to keep a smile on our face and a light in our heart. We can live every moment as if it were our last. He taught me arguably the most valuable lesson I could ever learn about the human capacity for self-transformation, which is essential to mastering the art of living with spontaneity.

The power to adapt to our circumstances and improve is encoded genetically in every human being on our planet. But it is the belief that you carry in your heart that will guide you in creating the life you want and becoming the person you want to be in this life. Regardless of any situation or circumstances, if you genuinely believe you have the ability to make choices for yourself, then you can make changes and better yourself because of those choices.

TWO

WE ARE HARDWIRED FOR HUMAN CONNECTION

Are you connected?

Things changed quickly soon after my dad died. I grew up. I wasn't a kid anymore, running home to watch cartoons and getting all excited about reaching first base with my girlfriend. I was going out with my friends to nightclubs and concerts, drinking vodka and tequila shots, smoking weed, and talking to many girls. At the age of seventeen, I got my driver's license, a full-time job, and my first car, a brand-new Chevrolet Cavalier. I worked hard, made money, and enjoyed the perks of living in beautiful Montreal. Soon I started college.

Being the first of my friends to have a car instantly made me the coolest one of my crew. Adding to my stature was that I was also the first of my friends to have a cell phone. My first phone was a shitty Nokia (not even a flip phone) that took way too long to send a text. Nothing like the smartphones we have today. No matter. It felt like life was beginning, and with a car, money to burn, and girls to meet, I was having a blast.

My first job was in a Greek restaurant. Before I became a waiter, leaving work with a few hundred dollars in tips in my pocket every night, I was a busboy. My very first night on the job, the restaurant was slammed, and I mean *slammed*, with a line out the door. I was wearing a white-collared button-up shirt and running around like a chicken without a head, feeling the uncomfortableness of sweat generated by carrying loads of baskets filled with dirty dishes to the back and bins full of ice to the front—going back and forth over and over again—dripping down my back and my armpits.

In a moment of relief during a five-minute break, I met the coolest guy ever, Alexander, a good-looking twenty-four-year-old college student from Russia.

Alex was as smooth of a talker as anybody I have ever met and just as nice. He was a waiter at the restaurant, and we met when I was trying to dry off in the back alley next to the exit. He came out for a smoke. Back then smoking cigarettes was still a thing, and restaurants were still half sectioned off for smokers and blanketed with cigarette smoke.

He didn't say a word or look at me, not at first. He pulled out a single smoke from the pack into his mouth in one swift move, no fingers, and then knocked a second one halfway out of the pack using his knuckle and offered it up to me.

"No, thank you," I said.

But he just stood there holding out the pack and looking at me. And well, I didn't want to be rude, so I took the cigarette. What can I say? It was my first day on the job, and I wanted to connect with the guy. He stuck out his hand and shook mine with a firm grip, introducing himself with a big smile on his face. "Alexander."

We chatted for a few minutes. You know, saying random shit: "Do you have a girlfriend?" "Are you in school?" "What are you studying?" "What do you want to do after school? "You see the game last night?" I assumed we were talking about the Montréal Canadiens. Some true-to-form, heart-to-heart conversation. While we were bantering, I found out we shared the same birthday, because it was coming up. Then we decided we would celebrate it together—instant male bonding.

Break time was over, so Alex finger-flipped his smoke to the ground and put it out with his wingtip shoe before heading inside. It was beautiful to watch. He stopped at the doorway and invited me to join him and a few guys from the restaurant for a beer after our shift. He took to me instantly, and I knew right away that we would become good friends.

Over the next few years, between working in the restaurant, being promoted to serving, making more money, going to college, taking periodic trips with friends to Cancun, Mexico, and saying goodbye to my teens, Alex and I become close, like brothers. We hung out often and had many deep conversations about life, and we celebrated every subsequent birthday together. In time, I began to date his girlfriend's best friend, and we went on many, many double dates.

Eventually, Alex moved on from the restaurant and we didn't see each other as often. We stayed close at first, but not as close as we had been when we worked together. He was going to Concordia University, as was I, but doing his own thing. He was still dating the same girl. However, I was no longer dating her best friend. I had new friends from school and a newfound passion for fitness training, so I spent more time in the gym hanging out with newer buddies who also loved to train.

Although Alex and I were focused on different things now, there was one thing that would never change between us. There wasn't a question about who we wanted to celebrate our birthday with—each other.

The last time Alex and I had chatted was a few months before the big day. We had confirmed that our plan was to be lining up vodka shots. I would be turning twenty-two. Alex would be turning twenty-nine. In that conversation, he told me he was under a lot of stress in school and wasn't sure about his program anymore. Also, he said he didn't have much time to see his girlfriend.

Adulthood seemed tough.

It was just after midnight on a weeknight less than three weeks before our birthday, when my phone rang. I was already sleeping. Alex wanted to talk some more.

At the time, I didn't think much of the conversation. He told me he would be leaving school for a few semesters to figure some things out. He had officially broken up with his girlfriend of three years although he loved her with all his heart. His voice sounded sad, but I didn't stay on the phone with him.

The truth is that it was late, I was tired, I had an early class the next morning, and I wanted to go back to bed, so I told him I would call him the next day and suggested he sleep off his distress. I felt sure that we would have a good heart-to-heart talk in the morning. The next day, however, when I reached out to Alex, I couldn't get a hold of him. He wasn't picking up his phone.

It was early morning the day after that. Close to 7 AM. I would be working the lunch shift at the Greek restaurant, so I didn't have to be there until 10 AM to do my usual cleaning before we opened. My eyes were still shut, and my head was comfortably tucked into my pillow when my phone rang next to me in a deep sleep. *Ugh. It's so early,* I thought.

"Yeah?" I said, eyes still closed. Head still comfortably tucked into my pillow. It was my boss.

"Danny," my boss said.

"Yeah."

"Listen, I have to tell you something."

"Yeah." Still half asleep.

"It's about Alexander. He jumped off the Champlain Bridge last night." And then I heard those two words again.

"He's gone."

AGAIN! Just like when my dad died.

I was in a complete daze and not exactly sure what I was hearing.

"Are you there?"

"Yeah." My eyes remained shut.

"Okay, I have to call other people." My boss got off the phone.

So, I should tell you that I have had, on rare occasions, vivid dreams that seem so real that I can feel every emotion connected with them as they are happening, and the moment I wake up, when I'm still half asleep, it doesn't feel like I've had a dream. In my mind, the dream has actually happened. Moments later, when I'm fully awake, I realize that it was, in fact, a dream the entire time though I'm often still feeling the emotion like I've had a real experience.

Sometimes the vivid dream is a good dream, an incredible dream, one that gives me moments to pause and connect to myself, like when I'm fully immersed into doing what I love or being in a place that makes me feel free and alive, and I'm sad that's it's not real, so I try to stay asleep and immersed. But sometimes, the vivid dream is a nightmare, like I'm falling, drowning, or having my heart ripped from my chest, and I don't know why it's happening or how I got there, but all I want to do is to wake up. I feel sure I'll die if I don't and my life will be over just like that. The moment I realize it's not real, I feel the biggest relief come over me.

I've had those dreams, every single one of them. But they're dreams, and I always get over them with time. That's what the call from my boss felt like, right then and there. None of my previous vivid dreams had been as intense as this one, but because I'd had my share of them, I thought it was plausible that this was a bad dream. I hoped it was.

I didn't want to open my eyes. I was going to give it a few moments. My thought was that when I had finally woken up, I'd realize that the call never happened. I was going to phone Alex, and he was going to answer, and I would hear his voice, and we would chat, and then we would meet up for coffee and talk about school and his girlfriend, whom I knew he loved and whom I knew loved him. And I would tell him his situation was not as bad as he thought.

I opened my eyes. There. The call had never happened. It was just a dream. I felt the horrifying emotion of it. I took a moment before I got out of bed to draw in a few very deep breaths, needing to let out even deeper breaths from my body.

I remembered the midnight call from Alexander two nights earlier when he had told me he felt down and confused. He had needed someone to talk to, someone just to be there. *I should have been there for him*, I thought. I called his phone and got his voicemail. I left him a message, telling him I was there for him and that we had let too much time pass between us, and I wanted to change that. Then I got myself dressed and ready for work, all the while thinking about the call and the dream I had just before I woke up. It was possibly the most palpable dream I had ever experienced. It was still lingering in my body, in my chest, in my mind. I needed to hear his voice.

I parked my car down the street from the restaurant and stayed in my seat for a few moments with my eyes closed. I took a few more deep breaths, hoping that I could remove the heaviness that was weighing down my body. It was 9:30 AM. I wanted this nightmare to pass.

Walking into the restaurant that morning, I saw my boss with his head buried between his arms behind the counter. He then slammed his fist against it. Two of my coworkers were sitting on a table by the entrance next to each other, one crying uncontrollably, the other comforting him with a look of disbelief on his face. This second guy got up and walked toward me, then put his hand on my shoulder and with a firm grip pulled me in. But I resisted his embrace and stood firmly against the door frame, pushing his hand off my shoulder. He didn't move. He stepped closer.

"It's just a dream," I said.

My friend looked at me with tears in his eyes and placed his hand back on my shoulder, gripping it tightly.

"No. No. It's just a dream, right?" I asked. And I repeated, "It's just a dream."

The third time I said it, tears were forming, and soon I sensed that I couldn't hold them back much longer. He pulled me into his chest and hugged me fully and tightly, and I said it one more time, "It's just a dream," before I completely let go.

It wasn't a dream. It was a nightmare. It was real.

Sitting with my coworkers, I felt a mix of painful emotions surface hard. Shock. Sadness. Despair. Anger. Horror. Guilt.

My mind was in a frenzy. I couldn't process what had happened. Thoughts were running all over my mind. *You don't just take your life! That's not supposed to happen.* I felt torn. I had lost my brother. He took his life, and he felt there was no other way.

I remembered Alex's call. That fucking call. *Why didn't I talk him through it? Why didn't I listen? Why didn't I see this coming?* Questions. And questions. And more questions. So many questions were running through my head. Clearly, he had been reaching out. I felt guilty that I had ended the call.

Alex was Jewish, so his body was buried the very next day. I don't remember much. It was the second funeral I attended before the age of twenty-two. The first being my father's, a man I didn't know well although he was my blood. By contrast, I knew Alex well even though he wasn't my blood. He was my best friend and brother, and I loved him deeply.

Here's what I do recall. The funeral looked like college graduation with close to a hundred twenty-somethings and tons of family present. Alex's father (whom I'd never met before) made sure he thanked every single person who came to pay their respects for his son, occasionally (more often than not) breaking down in tears with every hug he gave someone. When it was my turn, I told him, "Your son was my brother, and I feel your pain, and I am so sorry." I looked upon this man and felt my heart break with his. I was connected to him because I shared the tragedy of his loss.

Guilt and anger started to consume me. I was angry at Alex. I was angry at myself. I was angry at the world. I kept to myself for several days. My guilt didn't seem to go away, only to get stronger and burrow deeper inside me. I didn't say anything about how I was feeling to anyone, including my mom. When my friends from school would ask, "Why did he do it?" their question angered me because I did not have an answer.

I felt like a bomb whose fuse had been lit. An explosion became imminent a few nights later. I was working at the restaurant on an insanely busy dinner shift. *It is so busy that I don't even have time to cry, which is a good thing,* I thought. I needed not to think, just to do my work and get on with it.

Easier said than done.

Every little complaint— "My soup is too cold," "I ordered chicken souvlaki, not lamb," "My Coke is flat," "There's too much ice in my water," "What's taking so long with my food?" —was like having another little bit of my soul ripped from my body, having another little bit of my patience pushed past its limit. Someone was going to get punched.

I needed to get away from the chaos, even if it was for a single moment. I stepped out into the back ally next to the exit, the same spot where I had first met Alex. This fact didn't escape me. I stared down at the spot where he'd stood and remembered how he had swiped a cigarette out of the pack he gave me, the firm handshake, and the smile he gave me when he had seemed like the happiest guy in the world. It seemed like it was yesterday.

"Danny Boy." A friendly voice rang out from the door. My good friend John came out with a pack of smokes. He'd been working at the restaurant long before I started and was as close to Alex as anybody. We called him Skinner. Even till today, I have no idea why.

"Listen, a few of us are going to drive up to the mountains after we close up," he told me. "Smoke a joint, have a few beers, a few laughs. I think we all need a laugh."

"I heard. I'm good. But thank you," I said. I wasn't in the mood to be there. I didn't want to be near anybody or share any laughs. I wanted to try to make it through my shift without punching some asshole who kept bitching that his soup wasn't hot enough, and then leave.

"I know you're good, but you're going to come with us anyway," Skinner insisted.

"Why do you care?" I asked. Skinner never quite smoked an entire cigarette. He always tossed his butts on the floor after a few hauls.

He looked at me. Somehow, he knew what to say, possibly the only thing he could say, that I couldn't argue with: "Because I need you there." And that was all he had to say.

I looked away, momentarily, and smiled. "Okay," I said, turning to look at him. "I'll come." I knew that meant something and instantly I wanted to be there.

"Kalos," Skinner replied, which means "good" in Greek. "And stop slacking off out here, we're slammed in there." He always left the room with a joke.

It was about six of us. We took a few cars, a few six packs, and some weed and parked near an underground bridge. Another friend named John brought his guitar. We cracked open our beers and started reminiscing, telling old stories of Alex under the beautiful, clear night sky with the stars shining brightly in it above us. We had a few laughs, passed a joint around, had a few more laughs. Then John took out his guitar, pulled a few strings, feeling its tune.

Funny thing. As I watched him play his guitar, there was only one song I wanted to hear. I was thinking about it. I'm sure we were all thinking about it, but we didn't say what to play, and John didn't ask, he just played, fittingly, "Under the Bridge" by the Red Hot Chili Peppers.

It was a memorable night among good friends, saying goodbye to another dear friend, and captured perfectly by singing this song together. That song represented everything I was feeling. And I highly recommend you give a listen to the lyrics of this remarkably powerful ballad.

After the song, we sat there in complete silence. It was the most at peace I'd felt since getting the call Alex had jumped. With a beer in hand and a nicely rolled up joint being passed around, for a moment it felt like we were going to be okay.

It was still painful. Our good friend was gone. But we had each other. That was important for us. I didn't feel guilty anymore, and I didn't care anymore about how uncomfortable it was to feel so much pain or to cry for someone I loved so dearly. It was human.

I held that joint for a moment, staring into space. Tears from my eyes were slowly making their way down my face. I admit I'd thought Skinner was just saying he needed me there to get me to come, thinking it didn't really matter if I was there or not—maybe he needed me there, maybe he didn't. But he had known, although I would never have admitted it, that I needed him, and that mattered to him.

Skinner walked over and sat down next to me on the less-than-comfortable rock I was sitting on and put an arm around me. "Thank you," I told him.

"Danny Boy," he said. A slight pause followed before he asked me something that only he could ask me. "So, are you going to just keep holding that joint or are you going to pass it?" Even in a painful moment, he made me laugh.

What my friends did for me late that night was triggered by kindness and forgiveness. They helped me to open my eyes and see the light. That's where true kindness can come from. Times of pain and anger. Even in their darkest moments. I was there for every guy, and they were there for me. I felt blessed to be surrounded by that kind of love, support, and kindness.

Four Lessons Learned Through Loss

Here are four things I learned from this, my second experience of loss.

Lesson #1. Connection Embraces All Emotions

The biggest lesson in my loss was how powerful and healing our ability to connect can be. What does it mean to connect? Let's look at children's ability to connect. All a kid wants is to love and be loved. Even when they feel or sense any kind of pain or sadness from other people, they don't withdraw. They stay connected. Children accept these emotions without judgment or fear. Kids also experience incredible states of pure joy through their ability to connect with others. Acceptance is a quality of a spontaneous life.

Imagine being the adult that you are but still maintaining the ability to fully connect in the way that you did when you were a kid—no fears about it, no judgments, no voice telling you differently. Take all the responsibilities that you have today, be it with your family, your health, your career, and all your hopes and dreams. Imagine having a purpose that is guided by your powerful ability to connect with others. Wouldn't life be nice?

Lesson #2. Anger Limits Our Self-Awareness and Prevents Us from Thinking Logically

Anger confuses our sense of reality. It drives us into isolation. It's a dangerous, slippery slope to identify with our anger when we're grieving because it can lead us to believe we are bad for feeling bad. But anger doesn't make us bad people. Anger often comes from someone with a good heart.

Of course, you cannot know anger if you don't understand the flip side—and that's love. To get there, all you need to do is let go of the anger that is holding you back.

Lesson #3. Forgiveness Is a Choice

To forgive is liberating. It is the act of releasing the chains that are holding you in the past, which gives you the freedom to move forward. For me, those chains were anger and guilt.

Forgiving yourself and others is something that can only be experienced in the present, the moment you allow yourself to feel your pain and upset. Letting go of anger is to forgive, and to forgive is the ultimate switch from the past to right here, right now. The choice is always ours.

Start making it a practice to forgive.

Lesson #4. Kindness Is Healing

We each have our stories of times when kindness was either extended to us or we extended our own to someone else, and we know how both sides of the exchange feel. We see what kindness can do in emotional moments early on when we're kids growing up. We know where it comes from. And we know the positive effect that it instantly has on us. Sometimes we are kind simply because it's better than not being kind. Kindness influences everything.

It is my experience that kindness comes in small, random acts. As a tool for living, being kind to ourselves and others is one of our greatest superpowers. It comes with amazing benefits and yet it is a tool of which many people seem largely unaware. We really ought to continuously sharpen our ability to be kind, like we would sharpen a sword, to avoid it becoming dull and ineffective. Life is hard. School is hard. Work is hard. But being nice to people is easy.

THREE

WE BECOME WHAT WE FOCUS ON

Are you living intentionally?

The day I walked into a gym for the first time was a moment that defined the standards I would choose to live and succeed by, as well as the ones I still strive to teach others. The gym was a world where I would be introduced to methods to create a strong and powerful body, and in doing so, also to develop character, determination, and focus. Little did I know it, but I was destined to become a competitive bodybuilder.

Now, before I take you through my journey of building a champion's mindset and describing the preparation I did to become the best version of myself, I must ask you to observe how the road I traveled was paved with many failures, obstacles, and lots and lots of aha moments.

Let's rewind to the beginning. I was seventeen, and I didn't have an athletic gene in my body. I had an average build, and from the looks of my family history, I wasn't going to play point guard in the NBA or be a star running back in the NFL anytime soon—well, not unless I was ready to put in the work. Nonetheless, I did love sports, and I played hockey with my friends after school as often as I could. Gym class was my favorite class, especially when we played basketball and badminton.

Yes, I said badminton.

I didn't excel at any sport in particular, but I did carry with me the one fundamental that would be needed if I was ever going to understand the process of building strength and physical conditioning, and that was that I absolutely loved, loved, loved everything about playing sports: the competitive nature of it, the sense of being part of something greater, the absolute joy of the intensity with which the body feels and how that feeling permeates the mind and elevates the spirit.

It wasn't until I saw the infamous 1977 bodybuilding documentary *Pumping Iron* that I started to feel drawn to this new world of fitness. Bodybuilding was like a secret society of empowered people who were almost superhuman and sexy as fuck.

At the time, as we were transitioning into the twenty-first century, unlike today, a time when the culture of fitness has taken on a life of its own and is a billion-dollar industry and social media juggernaut, bodybuilding wasn't massively popular. Your typical cover models in magazines, either male or female, was skinny with absolutely no muscle definition. Average dudes played superheroes in movies—that is, except for the Muscles from Brussels (Jean-Claude Van Damme) and the Austrian Oak (Arnold Schwarzenegger). Not to say that Bruce Willis and *Die Hard* don't have a place in my heart due to my love of classic action films. They do. Let's get that straight. But Willis was no athlete.

Athletes were fast back then. Today athletes are not only fast, they're also strong, and they're big, and they can move as the body has never seen. Compare Michael Jordan's finesse on the basketball court in the 1980s and 1990s to LeBron James' sheer power now. Both with unbreakable mindsets.

The world was starting to change, and I was at the head of the line. My inspiration came in the form of one of my best friends in high school. Chris was the most popular kid in school, although, to be honest, he was kind of an asshole at times. Not to me, but his twistedly sarcastic sense of humor was well known to his friends and the rest of the school. He was the guy in the cafeteria who sat on the table and told stupid stories about stupid shit, and everyone listened. He also seemed to have no fear, literally; I saw him approach any girl, anytime, and say anything he wanted and never be fazed. We became good friends the day I joined the gym and saw him training, that is.

In school, Chris was the joker, the player, the goofball, and the guy who was good with numbers. He was remarkably good at math. The only guy I knew in high school who played the stock market. In the gym, he was focused and passionate.

Good looking, with long, slicked-back hair tied in a ponytail, he was jacked for a high-school kid. The gym was where we started talking. That was our common ground. But it wasn't so much the fact that he was there doing this thing that we both loved that made me want to be his friend, it was his reason why, when I found out the "why" later on, it got me curious and inspired me.

Chris was training for a bodybuilding competition. He was going to compete as a junior. *That's actually a thing?* I wondered. *I thought you had to be built like Arnold to do that kind of thing.* And yes, since watching *Pumping Iron*, I was all about the pump, and I understood what Arnold meant when he said the pump was exactly like "that satisfying feeling like I'm having sex with a woman and coming. Getting that feeling of coming in the gym," as he described it.[2] I was about it all, even when you consider I was still wet behind the ears on the subject for a guy in high school.

But yeah, Chris was no Arnold. Who was? His physique was a little closer to mine actually, and that opened my eyes to possibilities. After standing back and watching him train for a few weeks, in complete awe, while doing my workouts and learning to squeeze the muscle I was working and other fundamentals of training, just trying to put on size, secretly I began wanting to compete myself. I imagined stepping on stage in the best shape of my life—which doesn't say much being that I had only been training for a few months.

Chris' trainer was Rick Sparrow, a six-foot-three legend in the bodybuilding world, a former heavyweight competitor who had placed top three in all the major competitions in

Canada. Rick owned the gym. He had massive, detailed triceps unlike any I had ever seen. And I don't think even Arnold in his heyday had triceps like Rick's.

While the idea of approaching Rick felt intimidating, I thought, *What the hell?!* I was curious to find out what he thought about the idea of me competing, and honestly, what was the worst that could happen? Maybe he would laugh at me. I'd live. So, I did indeed approach him and asked him his thoughts about whether I had what it took to compete.

His response wasn't as bad as I thought it might be. He didn't laugh. He sized me up. Rick had a knack for knowing what someone weighed to the exact pound just by looking at him, a great skill for someone who has coached hundreds of fitness competitors, with the majority taking first or second place in their competitions.

Did I mention the massive trophy case in the gym covering six walls with three levels of shelves to each wall, filled with trophies, plaques, and medals, with framed photos accompanying each one, celebrating winners in various weight classes—men, women, tall, short, young, old—all champions in their respective categories? These awards symbolized each athlete's achievement and determination, dedication, grit, sacrifice, and sheer will to be the best. All had been trained by Rick or his brother.

Every time I looked upon the photos of these incredible physical specimens enshrined in their place on the wall as champions, I got chills running through every muscle that I barely had. I would feel myself unconsciously squeeze my biceps tightly and wonder what it would feel like to step on stage with my peers knowing what it took to get there.

Rick was a legend.

"Bring a hundred dollars tomorrow, and we'll get started." That was all Rick said. He was a man of a few words, but when he spoke, people listened. A hundred bucks, that seemed fairly cheap for training. I didn't really know what it was for, but I did as the man said, and even though we hadn't started anything yet, and really, although all I had intended to do was inquire, I said, "Hey, I want to compete, let's do this. I'm all in." It felt like there would be no turning back.

I wasn't quite sure what I was in for, but a feeling came up of fear and excitement, all blended into one spicy meatball lodged in the pit of my stomach.

The next day, I brought in a hundred bucks I'd saved up from three days' worth of hauling bins of dirty dishes and refilling water for Greek food-loving folks with bad garlic breath. Rick took my well-earned hundred-dollar bill and put it right into his pocket—not the cash drawer at the front desk, his pocket—then he took out a folder with two sheets of paper he'd made ready for me and handed it to me.

The first piece of paper was my workout plan, which consisted of things I had never heard off. Terms like *drop set, superset, reverse grip, slow negatives, front squats,* and *cardio* were on that page.

What the hell is cardio? I thought. I mean, I knew what cardio was, but doing thirty-minute sessions of it seemed tortuous, didn't it? *What the hell is a stair mill?* That didn't sound like fun.

Training was new to me. If only Instagram had existed back then, and I'd had other individuals and sources to reference, it might have been less daunting. We managed, but the internet was still slow and needed to be dialed up (yes, you required a phone line to get service), so resources were limited. Yeah, times were tough. Not quite as bad as black-and-white television before 1953 or the Great Depression of the 1930s, but annoying.

I was pumped. I wanted to learn. I wanted to experience some massive change and dive in headfirst. I wanted to pack on some serious muscle. And yes, I wanted to earn a place on the wall among the other super-athletic gym freaks and be looked upon as a super-athletic gym freak myself. I couldn't wait to get started.

The second sheet of paper was my seven-day meal plan. It read:

Meal 1: 8 egg whites, a cup of oatmeal, a glass of milk.

Meal 2: 6 oz chicken or steak, a cup of brown rice, a cup of greens.

Meal 3: protein shake.

Meal 4: same as meal 2.

Meal 5: same as meals 2 and 4.

And then there was my cheat meal: *Cheat meal?* Once a week, on Sunday, I could have an eight-ounce chicken breast, a plain baked potato, and one ounce of barbecue sauce. *THIS IS A CHEAT MEAL? SERIOUSLY?*

Mind you, as I was reading this sheet, I was still feeling the chocolate chip pancakes with real maple syrup digesting in my stomach that I had for breakfast about an hour before meeting with Rick. Well, I didn't think it was going to be easy.

Let's review.

Six months prior, I'd never set foot in a gym. I'd never followed any kind of diet/meal plan in my life. I'd never had any muscle gains. I'd never had to lose any kind of weight.

In the six months since I joined the gym, my only guidelines came from pictures in *Men's Health* and *Flex* magazines. Also, I'd like to draw a line in the sand and divide my life into BY and AY, meaning Before YouTube and After YouTube, referring to the tutorials at my disposal.

Oh, remember when I said I had a car and went clubbing, drank tequila, and talked to girls? Girls love tequila shots and being taken out for pizza, dessert, and brunch. Furthermore, I worked in a Greek restaurant, constantly surrounded by the smell of marinated lamb chops, steak, and chicken brochettes cooking on a fire grill, which I would partake of along with black forest cake and lemon pie. My Achilles' heel, of all things, was lentil soup, and ours was known in the entire city as the best lentil soup you will ever have. The idea of giving all these wonderful foods up was a scary prospect.

Discipline was foreign to me. I seek comfort, even when I have to work. As a high school and college student, I always did my homework with the television on, for example.

There are words I've often heard in passing, usually from teachers and guidance counselors. Sometimes in casual conversation about the future, when they want me to know,

I can be anything I want to be. But because my mind was somewhere else, until I had to learn discipline in the gym, I never gave them much thought. The words were:

Sacrifice.

Determination.

Belief.

Mental toughness.

Focus.

Resilience.

Commitment.

I was not there yet with any of them, but when Rick handed me his two handouts, I felt excited about what would happen through committing.

I had always been of the mindset of having fun, playing sports, and enjoying healthy competition; having friends; being part of something cool, and having a routine. I loved my routines. Even before I took up bodybuilding, instead of doing the things that most of my friends were doing, such as staying up late at night drinking and partying, I had established healthy habits. Although I didn't know it at the time or as clearly as I understood it later, the words listed above would inform my thoughts and actions. They would define the values I would need to live by: the standards of excellence that I needed to uphold and embrace to set myself apart as a competitor.

I had three months to get myself down from 172 to 154 pounds and try to pack on as much muscle as I could humanly do. Three months to see what I was made of.

Easy peasy, I foolishly thought.

My journey was just beginning. And I had no real idea what I was in for. Understatement of the year! I'd never gone through anything like Rick's training program before in my life, and the coolest thing about it was that I was doing it with my friend. Chris and I were set to compete against each other in the same category—same age, same weight class—in a contest where only one person leaves the stage with the first-place trophy. Which was cool because I knew Chris would push me to work even harder, and I would use him as my standard.

Chris had months of preparation ahead of me and a year of training to my six months. He was already looking sharp. As for me, I was still digesting those pancakes as I read the handout telling me about my new spartan diet. If I had known that the delicious pancakes I had that morning would be the last ones for a while, I would have had a second helping. But it's probably better that I didn't.

Competing against Chris didn't bother me. I wasn't in it for the first-place trophy, as damn cool as winning it would have been. I wanted to train for other reasons, the same reasons that had me looking past the three months of preparation. I was thinking, *Is this possibly something that could become my future?*

I went to the store that day and got all the food and other supplies I needed to get. For instance, I bought myself a food scale so I could measure everything. I packed it all separately, putting meat and veggies in the freezer, eggs in the fridge, and oatmeal in the cabinets the first time I meal prepped. Funny story, I even thought about what a great business it would be to start a meal prep company, the first of its kind. *Imagine all the people who don't have the time to cook. Nobody is doing it.*

I goofed on bypassing that idea, didn't I? Fresh, ready-to-home-cook meals in boxes have become a huge business in the past few years.

I started training with Chris. Doing so allowed me to push myself harder than I would on my own. Every single workout felt like I was training within an inch of my life because Chris was training within an inch of his life. I couldn't slack off because I knew he was taking it seriously. It was incredible to watch my body slowly change. This transformation inspired me to train even more, and my motivation to change my physique also was steering me forward.

In that first month when I got started, I found my passion and more, not only something that I loved doing, but something I sensed that I could be good at, or even great at.

The lifestyle I committed myself to was new, yet I was learning quickly. As remarkable as the physical transformation was once it started becoming noticeable, the feeling I had was something else. I felt a sense of determination, a sense of hunger. Something that would serve to fuel me.

But food was a different story.

At the beginning, trying to stuff plain, tasteless oatmeal and egg whites down my throat every morning while taking a multivitamin and mineral pack that consisted of eleven thumb-sized pills was mentally exhausting. As I was presented with this challenge, three months seemed like an eternity. Although I was excited to go at it strongly, my resolve was weak. Also, it was summertime, so when the opportunity to go out with friends arose, I would say yes, each time telling myself it would be the last time. *Just this one last time and then no more.* Why? Because it was a break I wanted to use as a distraction from it all.

My excuse for my lack of resolve was that I needed more time to get myself mentally prepared to follow the "crazy, asinine" meal plan Rick had recommended. As a result, a cheat meal wasn't a cheat meal; it was a cheat day. My barbecue chicken with an ounce of sauce and a plain baked potato on the side was more like a chicken burger and large poutine, which is a plate of fries covered with cheese and gravy—a favorite in the city of Montreal.

And Domino's Pizza and cookie dough ice cream.

And Saturday nights were spent out with the boys.

Chris was there too, that damn instigator! I didn't want to say no as I didn't want to miss out. I had FOMO (fear of missing out) before the term *FOMO* existed. I just always kept telling myself, *One more time. This will be the last time.*

The first month came and went, and we were down to two months left until the big day, and I thought I still had enough time to prepare to be my best. The days and early morning got harder. Waking up got harder, and the cardio sessions were brutal. I set my alarm for 5 AM so I could do my cardio sessions first thing in the morning on an empty stomach and get them out of the way. But that was if I even got up. I had become a snooze-button specialist, mastering the fine art of hitting the button with my eyes closed and staying in bed. I either knew exactly where my hand needed to slap or was so deeply asleep that the alarm just kept going off until my mom walked in the room and shut it off.

I thought I just wanted another five more minutes of shut-eye, but what I really wanted was to take a time machine and go to the end of every cardio session, when it was done. When I did get up, I dragged myself to the gym—barely.

With the drastic weight drop that came from eating plain food (despite all my cheating), my training got even more intense. Then the things in the gym I had started to love doing so much become the things I couldn't wait to get over. The training was like a nagging girlfriend I couldn't get rid of.

Then there was the restaurant and its busy nights, which were every night, and the process of climbing the stairs to the second floor on my tired post-workout legs. I was constantly going up and down during four- to five-hour shifts, fatigue setting into my body, and blanketing my mind. Many nights I thought, *How terrible would it be if I snuck away and had one or two bowls of lentil soup?* One bowl, heavy on the cream base and overly salted with tons of flavoring. Not at all part of the meal plan. Just me pushing myself many steps back from my commitment. Where was my passion then? Where was my drive? Why was I doing this to myself?

Then insomnia kicked in, and every night I contemplated quitting.

Every morning I did the same as well.

Then came the final six weeks of my training regimen, and I had to get serious about it. I was losing weight because I stuck to the diet during the week for the most part, although I have a vague recollection of sleepwalking in the middle of the night and eating chocolate chip cookies from the kitchen cupboard. Why were those even there?

The cardio sessions had become even more brutal, and really, it was my fault. Rick increased my cardio time as the show approached, quite possibly because of all the shit I was secretly eating too close to the date.

I knew.

He knew.

And I just kept thinking about those seven words again, questioning what each meant.

Sacrifice? What does that mean?

Determination? What does that mean?

Belief? What does that mean?

Mental toughness? What does that mean?

Focus? What does that mean?

Resilience? What does that mean?

Commitment? I don't even care anymore.

I'd paid one hundred dollars to see what I was made of, and I was made of chocolate chip cookies, alcohol, and lentil soup. I wanted to give up so many times, not because the training was hard, but because I didn't know what the hell I was doing. Why couldn't I keep myself focused and committed? This was supposed to be fun. Right? Where was my resilience?

Then, as I approached the 163-pound mark, with mere weeks left to go, I was going to face new struggles. The first struggle was the challenge of cutting carbs out of my diet. This meant drastically eliminating my body's main energy supply to ensure the remaining weight was taken off efficiently while keeping as much muscle as possible. This stage gradually begins a few weeks before a competition so a bodybuilder can start adding the necessary muscle definition. Bodybuilders get judged on how ripped they are. What soon followed was even going to be harder than I ever imagined, the water-cutting stage, the final hurdle every bodybuilder must endure to make that final weigh-in. By starting to completely cut off any source of hydration days before the show, you are creating a more vascular composition to the physique.

I don't want to sound blasphemous, but I genuinely felt like Moses must have when he was walking the desert for forty years with his band of escaped slaves. Parched.

Finally, I reached my desired weight, and the day of the competition came. I'd lost nearly twenty pounds, and done so without going diet crazy, right, with a few cheats here and there, and a few more midnight indulgences. So, great, right? *Hmmm?*

Remember, a year before I'd never walked into a gym, I'd never lifted a dumbbell, and I'd never thought I would be where I was on this day. I was about to step on stage wearing a shiny blue bathing suit in front of hundreds of people, including friends, family, strangers, and other incredible athletes, everyone there to see what six months of training and three months of questionable dieting looked like on me.

There's a scene in *Pumping Iron* when Arnold is on the Mr. Olympia stage in 1970, posing, smiling, having the time of his life, and he knows he has won. He knew it wasn't even close. He had a standard, and by keeping to his standard, he came in as the best weightlifter the world had ever seen. The other guys looked incredible, and they upheld a standard too. And backstage they were all having fun.

And what of me? I was tired—flat-out exhausted—and all I could think about was the liter of water and box of cookies I had stashed in my bag downstairs in the locker room and all the candy bars I had hidden in a shoebox in my room back home.

It was pretty cool to be up there on stage next to my friend. Ours was a pretty heavy weight class. I remember there being about ten guys in our category. I was still in the best shape of my life, but I wasn't in the best shape I could have been, and I knew it. And Rick knew it. The months of work I'd put into my preparation, including the cardio sessions I missed and the extra meals I ate were all on display there.

You can cheat yourself, but you can't cheat the results.

I took eighth place. Chris won the show. I knew he'd won even before they announced the placings. The entire experience left me disappointed, to say the least, but not my placing. I knew I got what I earned. I was disappointed in myself and what I had brought to the table.

I learned a few things about myself, and those words my teachers used to preach to me. I now had tangible evidence that what you focus on, you bring into your life. The problem for me was that I had fixated on the results and the achievement, and the whole time I'd rarely thought about the journey.

Fast Forward to Four Years Later

I lived in the gym pretty much every day for the next four years, and the way my body changed in size and condition was quite noticeable. I was strong and lifting serious amounts of weight by then. I won't go into listing all my max reps for squats and bench presses and so on because it's not important. What stands out and matters to me is that in the four years after that show, my mindset changed. I elevated my standards and developed a level of self-reliance and dedication that started to affect other areas of my life in positive ways. After four years of training, I was a very happy 190 pounds, bigger than Chris, and even stronger too.

A lot had happened in the four years that followed my eighth-place finish. And even more happened after that. I was now a university student and enthusiastic journalism major, studying writing—and a gym addict or muscle head, or whatever you want to call me, with a fire inside my gut for training.

A few changes stand out as I look back on this period. I had moved on from my first restaurant job to work at a higher-class restaurant that sat nearly 250 people and was packed nightly. I was making almost $200 a night as a server and started being very smart with my money, saving as much as possible. In my heart, I knew I needed to prepare myself to eventually move on from where I was, possibly moving to new cities, possibly to new countries. Due to the condition of my body, some modeling agencies in New York were scouting me. I flew to spend a weekend there and visit with them. But I wasn't ready yet to move on.

A few things were still heavy on my mind, including Alexander's death. Following his suicide, I took some time off school to figure things out. This allowed me to work and save more. If I wasn't working, I was in the gym getting stronger, pushing myself harder, focusing on areas to improve, and putting my mind and heart on what I loved to do.

I had fallen in love with the training, the pain, and the preparation of competitive bodybuilding. I loved watching my body change the way it did. I had fallen in love with the constant satisfaction of self-improvement.

As my standards changed, my focus changed. All the little rituals and habits in my life changed. Yet I did not know how much it all would mean when I competed again, and it got hard. What would happen once the pain became real, and sacrifices were necessary? How much character would I have in moments when new challenges appeared?

Would I ever get to the point that every champion gets to, the point where it is decided who will prevail and who will come up short? The point that is decided by answering who is hungrier? Who wants it more?

I knew another show was coming up in a few months. Fifteen athletes from the gym were getting ready to compete in this upcoming show, divided into many different classes of weight and different age groups. Rick was overseeing every single person, including weigh-ins, poses, and choreographed routines.

It was an early afternoon, and the gym was quiet. I was training near the stretching area next to the trophy cases that had doubled in size and trophies since my eyes first looked upon them. I stood there catching my breath, taking a moment between sets, looking at a picture of myself hanging on the wall, my medal underneath it, not even inside the glass casing. I was holding an abdominal and quadricep pose with my arms stretched fully behind my head and my left leg sticking forward, the foot resting on my toes, while I was trying to flex as much as I could in both muscle areas. The area below my navel in my abdominals was slightly bloated, and my legs barely had any muscle definition. It looked smooth like a baby's ass. I recognized that I could thank midnight chocolate chip cookies and Dairy Queen Blizzards for those results. And I looked at my peers whose images were encased in the glass, shredded and defined. Each had a smile on his face (with a few exceptions) that said it all.

After Alex's death I had wanted to lose myself in an activity, one that would require every part of me, including my heart. And I'll tell you, despite having a bad taste in my mouth after the first competition, sticking with the training and signing up to do another competition wasn't a hard decision for me.

I saw Rick sitting behind the desk watching something on the television. I walked up to the counter. "Rick?"

He didn't turn around. "Yup," he said. You've got to respect a man of a few words.

"I was thinking . . . I should compete again."

He still didn't turn around.

"Should?" he responded. He was also a man who needed you to be specific with him when you told him something.

"My apologies," I said, clarifying, "I *want* to compete."

He still didn't quite turn around, just looked over his shoulder right at me. "It's about time." Then he turned his head back to his show.

And he said one more thing: "Bring a hundred bucks tomorrow."

Developing a Champion's Mindset

If you're interested in developing a champion's mindset, here are some tips.

1. Ask, "What's my why?"

The biggest difference between the first time I competed, and the second was not my muscle maturity. It was that I knew *why* I was training. I understood my motivation. This time my why fit my standards and it fit my desire to do my best no matter what I was doing.

Your *why* is what separates you from everybody else who is going after the same thing you are. If you prevail, it's because your why got you there. If you stay up nights looking at the stars, thinking about it and you can't focus all day because your why is bigger than everything else that presently stands in your way, you will find the determination and commitment to achieve it.

What does it mean for you to see yourself in this journey you are living to reach the levels to which you have aspired? How will this change your life? How will it change you?

Know your why to begin developing the mindset of a champion.

2. Set Clear Goals and Have an Execution Plan

The morning after I declared my intent to compete, I didn't have chocolate chip pancakes with real maple syrup. In fact, I couldn't remember the last time I'd had pancakes. I woke up early, fresh, and with a burst of energy that I hadn't felt in a while.

That day I met with Rick and got a new workout and meal plan. The phrases *Easy* and *I got this* didn't come to mind, but *Challenge accepted* did.

Now, I'll tell you. I was initially of the mindset that being 190 pounds and already pretty shredded I would compete in the light heavyweight division, just north of 180, which wouldn't require too much weight loss. Rick had a different idea. And he made his point very clearly. He said, "If you compete as a light heavyweight, I can't say for sure that you will win the competition. But if you compete as a lightweight, then I can guarantee that you will."

Remember, Rick never made false claims or said anything unless he felt there was a reason to say it. Lightweight is 154 pounds. Reaching the same weight as the previous contest would mean I was looking at dropping thirty-six pounds in three months. I knew what this meant. I knew what I had to do, what was at stake, and what I would endure.

Rick gave me the option not to do it, but honestly, that wasn't an option for me. Having made my decision, Rick and I planned out each month—what my diet looked like, how it would change, the intensity required in my training, and the cardio sessions.

The lengthy training period wasn't about winning; it was about giving my best every day, and about having a purpose. And that reason alone was going to get me out of bed every morning, the passion and drive I had meant that nothing could stop me.

You can't just know what you want. You must know what is needed of you in every step of the way if you're going to achieve the unthinkable. If you're going to be successful, you'll have to do what only a mere percentage of the world is doing. Do not waste a single second of your twenty-four hours. Know what you need to do and set a plan. By setting a plan, you will be preparing yourself better to handle any situation. Setting a plan keeps your mind more organized and creates the mindset to stay focused on the goal.

3. Surround Yourself with People Who Inspire You and Push You Forward

Training with Chris the first time I competed allowed me to push myself more than I would have ever pushed myself had I gone it alone. I didn't have the same standards back then as the second time I competed, but the whole experience was a useful starting point. I progressed well after that first show and built the little habits and rituals of success along the way.

In bodybuilding, as in life, you can do things on your own. This is an option. And maybe you are the best and finish first every single time you do what you do, so you don't need support. If that's the case, then you ought to write a book that inspires millions of people who want to thrive similarly. Or, like I did when I wanted to be serious about training, you can find someone that gets the best out of you. We are always growing, moving, and changing; that's what life is, constant motion. Even in presence and stillness, we are in constant change. And we often need help to navigate the process of growing. Those who are expert in a subject can help you to develop a championship mindset.

The second time I decided to compete, I started training with my friend Norm, a guy I'd met at that first show. He competed in a different category than me and not only did he win his division and pretty much blow everybody away with his incredible muscle definition and symmetry, but he also became a legend the moment he stepped on stage for his sixty-second choreography routine. He moonwalked onto the stage to Michael Jackson's "Billie Jean." Norm won Best Posing Routine, a plaque given to only one male and one female competitor among the hundreds that compete.

Every evening I would drive forty-five minutes to train with Norm at his gym. I started lifting with more intensity. I discovered a new threshold of pain, a new level of mental and physical "push" that I could only develop by training with Norm.

The people you decide to surround yourself with are sharing and affecting your energy. The question is, are they taking or giving energy? The body is all energy, and our surroundings motivate that energy. We can fall backward by hanging with the wrong crowd. We can surround ourselves with negative people and allow them to drain our energy. Or we can choose to fall forward by working and spending time with people that push us forward. People with knowledge. People who have mastered what you desire in your life.

The true champion adopts the mindset of learning, and chooses whom he or she learns from wisely. The champion is also wise about who is given their energy. Will they matter in five years?

4. Train Your Mind

If you want to be a champion, everything comes down to the choices and decisions you make.

In my case, the first month of training—three months out from the show—was the easiest, allowing me to adapt to all the changes I was making in my routine. Waking up early, I would get in a cardio session, which was a mere thirty minutes in the morning on an empty stomach. I also began preparing all my meals in advance. This enabled me to match my behavior to my determination.

When I was down to two months preshow, training was more intense. My regimen included longer cardio sessions, I cut calories and carbs from my diet and made little changes to my workouts, such as adding more drop sets. Now fatigue started to show up, a little bit more every week.

I had a memorable moment one night, with about a month to go. I woke in the middle of the night at around two in the morning, and I couldn't get back to sleep, so I made my way downstairs to the kitchen. I sat on the floor across from the fridge with my knees tucked into my chest, hands crossed over them, just staring at it. I believe I was close to 170 pounds at the time, which was my original starting weight when I was seventeen. On this evening, it was twenty pounds less than the weight I had started out carrying. I knew I still had sixteen pounds to go to make my weight class, pounds which would come off easily once I cut my carbs and water.

Up until this point, I had done everything the way I was supposed to. There were no cheat days, no sleep-ins, no dates with girlfriends, no parties, and no skipping workouts. As Rick had planned, my weight was coming off as it was supposed to, everything was being executed the exact way he'd designed it.

I was thinking about the food in the fridge. There wasn't any junk food in the house, just good stuff: fruits and vegetables, hummus and carrot sticks. And I wasn't craving junk food. But what wouldn't I give for an apple? For a slice of pineapple? I wasn't starving myself per se, but I was following an extremely strict meal plan.

I was anticipating the hard leg workout awaiting me in the morning. My legs felt like toothpicks carrying a duffle bag filled with cinder blocks. My energy was questionable, and I was emotionally tied to my body. My mind started to ask me questions, like:

Why am I doing this?

Is this too hard?

Can I keep going?

And then those seven defining words started to appear again with new questions that took my energy to a higher level. I was essentially coaching myself to stay on course.

Sacrifice. Will I choose to sleep for five more minutes in the morning or will my goals wake me? Will I choose to go out with my friends one more time for one more drink or will I choose to be strong over being seen? Will I choose girls, eating more calories, and taking more days off, or will I favor what I must do over what I want to do when it becomes harder to do it? What does it mean to me not to give up or give in for the ultimate pursuit of my goal?

Determination. What is my purpose? What gets me out of bed every single day? What gets me excited? What advantages do I have and can I use in every moment? How is what I'm doing aligning with what I want? What can I do to work as hard as I can?

Belief. What am I telling myself every morning when I wake up? What is my truth? What am I telling myself when the pain gets real, and the work gets harder? What drives my faith?

Mental toughness. Do I still live by the standards I developed for my period of training? Do I have emotional stability that drives every decision? Am I staying objective? Can I adapt to my environment? Can I adapt to change?

Here I was reminding myself that I always have a choice: Never. Give. Up.

Focus. Do I always know where my focus needs to be? Where are my thoughts going? Are my thoughts guiding my actions?

Resilience. Is my work ethic unbreakable? Will I be able to stick with my training and commitments even when I feel like I could falter?

Everything in life is a lesson. It is, therefore, important for us to remind ourselves that things will get hard. We must know our strengths and never be afraid to use them. Every obstacle and adversity ultimately will make us stronger.

My next question led to a discovery.

Commitment. Do I care?

Yes, I did care!

Having a championship mindset means we must stay inspired. Stay motivated. Believe anything is possible and never settle. Remember, we have no limitations. I haven't met you, but I can promise you that you are stronger than you know. You are not average. You will be relentless as long as you remember your why.

5. Speak Affirmations

We can train the mind beyond its present limits by choosing words that link it to strength rather than pain. If you repeatedly tell yourself, "It's too hard" and "I can't do this," this is what your mind will believe. Your negative thoughts will manifest in actions like quitting early, sleeping late and skipping morning cardio, or deviating from your meal plan. By focusing on positive assertions that tell you how much you want and deserve to achieve your goals, you are reinforcing that you're strong enough. You are training your mind to give you what you want.

In the kitchen in the middle of the night, as I was staring at the fridge, I told myself:

I am strong.

I am powerful.

I am focused.

I am a champion.

I have what it takes.

I am disciplined.

I do not feel pain.

Then I let go of all the negative thoughts I was having and allowed myself to be there in that moment, in the middle of the kitchen at two in the morning. All of a sudden, it wasn't hard anymore to resist my desire for food. I didn't feel pain. I felt every cell inside me awaken with every word I uttered in my mind, with every deep inhalation and exhalation. I was allowing myself to feel the experience of that moment.

The truth is that one apple would not have done any real damage to me physically. I probably could have had it, walked into the gym the next day, and my weight would have been the same, and Rick would have looked at me and never known the choice I'd made.

But it did matter that I skipped the apple because that choice represented the decision I had made three months earlier to build everything I was building in this journey.

Eating the apple would have been like telling myself, *You're off the hook.* Then what about the next night and the one after that?

And what would have happened if one apple became two, and two apples became a piece of bread, a slice of cheese, or a chocolate bar? It would have been harder to draw a line and believe I meant it.

With each breath, the words *sacrifice, resilience, mental toughness,* and *belief* (meaning belief in myself) initiated a very powerful turn of my mindset.

I don't know what it was at that moment that helped me keep my commitments going. It wasn't the show that I was thinking about. It was deeper. It was something about just that moment being there, feeling every cell awaken and transform. I got up from the floor and went back to bed. Through the night, I stayed connected to each word, and I reinforced my intention with my breathing.

I had a few more nights like that one. Each one, the same as the other, breathing deeply and connecting the words *strong* and *powerful* to the feelings of joy and purpose, visualizing, and connecting mentally to my why.

Words are powerful. The words we think become the beliefs we live. Think about the words that you want people to see in you. Think about the words you want to embody. Are you a true testament of those words? Affirm who you are in your head. Repeat those words in your mind first thing in the morning and at various times in the day. Allow them to begin to frame your mindset.

6. Enjoy the Experience

The big night came. I was waiting below the stage with all the other competitors. Everybody had their own ways of getting ready, some pumping themselves up by doing pushups and bicep curls, a few by meditating in the corner, and others by chatting with their coaches. It was a big show, with what looked like hundreds getting ready to step on stage. The number of friends, family members, spectators, and sponsors in the auditorium was even higher. I had Norm by my side, my close friend and training partner, and the guy who also helped me design my posing routine.

Rick came up to me and pointed across the locker room to a young guy with massive legs and told me he was in the same class as me, and he would probably be my biggest competitor. However, I didn't see it that way. I didn't view anyone as a competitor. I saw myself as my biggest competitor.

Four years earlier, I beat myself. I. Beat. Myself. I gave in to my excuses. I allowed myself off the hook. When the work started getting hard, I gave in.

That evening, before I even stepped on stage, I had already won because I came in being the best version of myself. I'd done everything I promised myself I would. When I looked back over the three months of preparation and all the sleepless nights when I sat staring at the fridge at 2 AM, and the sacrifice of all the things I said no to; and when I recalled how the workouts got hard and the cardio sessions got worse, yet I made the decision to keep going, I knew I had already won.

Of course, I won't pretend that I didn't want to win when I was called for the final three at the awards ceremony. After calling out the third-place finisher, it all came down to me and the guy Rick had pointed to in the locker room. In a moment I'll never forget, I held my breath for just a second and closed my eyes before they announced that second place went to—and his name was called, not mine. I won't pretend that I didn't jump for joy and that tears didn't run down my cheeks.

It was an incredible moment of achievement and reflecting on it in hindsight I can only say that the entire experience, all of it, was just as satisfying as the one I had that night.

But (and I love when there's a *but)* it wasn't quite over for me that night. Thanks to working with Norm, who has kick-ass dance moves and choreography skills, I not only went home with first place in the lightweight category, but I also won Best Posing/Dance Routine in the show. Norm inspired me through his work ethic and physical conditioning, which were as solid as I have ever seen on anybody.

Who knew I could dance?

Nothing else matters in what you do in life more than if the thing you are working so hard to achieve is the thing that is setting a fire in your soul. If you recognize that and you come through hard times and struggle and you will, let that fire in your heart create joy from your struggles as your struggles is what ultimately will build the mindset of a champion. When you look back and remember what got you where you are, all the failures and rejections, remember that this made you. Enjoy every moment along the way. Keep telling yourself that this is all part of the story of how you are moving towards the life you want.

No matter what your goal is—and I would not assume that you are a bodybuilder like me—your mind is either your biggest asset or your biggest liability. The thoughts that tell you, *I can't*, must be supplanted with thoughts that tell you, *I can*. You likely will go through ups and downs, feel pain, endure setbacks, and doubt yourself if you are stretching to accomplish something meaningful and bigger than you've ever done before and what you tell yourself in all moments of challenge is what counts.

If you don't cultivate the mindset that the bigger picture is what matters, as opposed to feeling good mattering most, then you will do things to avoid your discomfort. Tell yourself that every little moment along the way matters and is significant, that the entire journey matters.

Remind yourself often that if you connect to your "why" and let go of your "I can't," then you have already won. As long as you make an honest attempt to reach your goals, you are always winning, no matter what the outcome. This is how you will find out who you genuinely are. Each contest is but a steppingstone in this great thing called life.

FOUR

WE CAN BECOME OUR OWN MENTORS

Are you self-sufficient?

When we're kids, we have the protection of our parents and count on them to make 95 percent of our decisions for us. During our teens and early adulthood, we pick up new responsibilities. Nothing quite kicks off our life education like having to take accountability for every area of our lives and provide for ourselves in every way imaginable without the shield or input of our parents. Welcome to adulthood, to living on our own and being completely self-sufficient. As we make and then learn from our mistakes, we develop a better sense of self and become more competent.

I frequently think about the kid I was growing up, escaping into my dreams that seemed destined to remain dreams. I was lost in my childhood, many times thinking I was dealt a bad hand and struggled to find my way through life's turmoil and confusion into my early twenties. Then I put forth some effort to chase my dreams and conditions in my life began to shift.

Whether we know it or not, we are all students of life. Like any other students, our education starts in the classroom with a subject and a lesson, a book, and a page. In the higher learning of life, each moment or incident, each conversation or circumstance is a lesson. At times we may not quite understand or see what the subject is. But there always is one. And the clue to what it is has to do with the nature of our desires.

The ultimate degree to which we self-actualize each lesson is relative to the degree of how self-aware we are. We are always students because the mind's capacity to learn doesn't end. However, there will be a switch, and one day, we will also become our own teachers. It is part of our evolution. The momma cub doesn't want to let go of her baby cub, but the time will come when the baby cub must fend for himself. In this new reality, we will use what we've learned to make our own hard choices.

I was coming off the challenging three-month character-building journey of planning out every little detail of my life, including meals, workouts, and weigh-ins, that led up to my inspiring first-place finish on the bodybuilding stage. This crowning achievement had taught me what I could do in the face of extreme mental and physical obstacles if I adopted the right kind of perseverance and mindset. I was on a high.

I was in the best shape of my life and had a good amount of savings put away. Having decided to take a year off from university, I was starting to think about what was next. Now working full time again as a server in a restaurant, one incredible conversation set a new dream in motion.

Late one afternoon, while readying my section of tables for another busy evening shift by doing small chores like filling the salt and pepper shakers, I got to chatting with the sweetest couple you could imagine. Tom and Cindy, an American couple who were visiting their grandkids from Arizona, were both in their sixties, well-traveled, and had a very happy marriage. I make this last observation because, well, in my experience, I haven't seen many couples that are so happy spending time together after being married to each other for so long. It was a refreshing change.

"Tell me about yourself, Danny." It seemed like it would lead to a normal conversation when Tom asked me that question.

Where do I start? I thought. "What would you like to know?" I asked as I placed their waters on their right sides, just above the table setting, as servers are taught to do.

"You're young and good-looking," Tom replied, "there has to be more to you than serving steak and ribs."

Having finished cleaning the majority of my section, I had all the time in the world, which doesn't often happen once the dinner rush begins. I explained that I had taken some time off from school and that I was working and saving.

And because it was fresh in my mind, I also told them about winning awards at the bodybuilding competition.

"That's incredible. Good for you. What are you saving for? What's your master plan?" they asked.

I thought this was a loaded question. I never really had looked at my dreams before as a "master plan," but I had goals that got me excited and made me feel alive. I told them about my dreams of acting and storytelling. "I've always wanted to go to New York and become a great actor. I was there once, for modeling, but it wasn't the right time."

Let's put this exchange in perspective. Some conversations come and go in life—well, the majority of them come and go. This one has stayed with me even fifteen years after that day. It was as lifechanging a conversation as any I've ever had, and I've had quite a few of them.

Tom told me a little about Cindy and himself. He had fought in the Vietnam War. He was with the U.S. First Platoon when the war broke out, and although he didn't seem particularly fond of discussing that part of his life, he did because he was making a point. "I saw friends of mine die fighting a war people didn't understand. I finally got home after my service, and instead of being seen as a hero serving my country, they called me a baby killer.

"I became angry. I got myself a Harley, let my hair grow long, and took off on the open road. I was living that *Easy Rider* life. Then one day, I went to a monastery in Seattle, and it changed my life. I left there, and I left all my anger there with it.

"And that's when I met Cindy."

I was glued to every word Tom spoke and completely forgot about the rest of my duties. Anytime someone in the kitchen called out "Runner to pick up food," it was like a faint voice in the background.

Tom continued, "I had a dream. It was a vision. I always wanted to build a successful, family-owned restaurant I could leave to my kids. One day, Cindy and I were driving cross country, and we came upon this mom-and-pop diner that was for sale. I looked at Cindy and immediately told her, 'We're going to live here.' And I made an offer to buy it for cash.

"And that was that. For the next ten years, we lived above the restaurant rent-free, and started a great business that my three sons are running today."

Intermittently excusing myself to take orders and check back with a few tables as other diners were slowly walking in and being seated, I came back when I could for a few minutes at a time to continue the conversation. "I'm going to tell you two hard truths, Danny . . . ," Tom said.

The first hard truth: "A dream means nothing unless you have the heart to see it through. And I'll tell you something, Danny. I've seen everything. Everything you can imagine. I've been through it all. I've seen death stare at me, had friends die in my arms. I've died myself, and they brought me back. I shit you not! I've been through the unimaginable.

"Listen to me carefully. The worst thing you could ever do for yourself is if one day when you get to be my age, and you look back, and you carry a sense of regret. It'll hit you like a dagger through the heart. You have one life. Having a dream already puts you way ahead of the game."

The second hard truth: "What you want to do in life and what you think you'll be doing ten years from now will most likely change. Life changes, your path changes, you change. But that doesn't matter. The only thing that matters is that right now you're going after what you want and what makes you happy."

The restaurant had started to get busy, and I nearly had a full section as I was preparing Tom and Cindy's bill. I placed it on the edge of the table. "Listen, no rush. Stay as long as you want. And thank you, it was a real pleasure meeting both of you. You gave me a lot to think about.

"I look forward to seeing you again."

Tom took the bill and slid it under his arm, then gave me one last farewell set of words. "Danny, I hope I don't see you here again."

I understood.

That concluded our conversation.

Throughout the next few days, all I thought about was what Tom told me. His words were imprinted on my brain. I started asking myself questions: *So, what is holding me back?* I didn't have an answer. *What am I afraid of?* I didn't have an answer. *How much more do I need to save?* I had plenty to get started. *So, now what?*

I jotted down a list of what I needed to do: There was a talent agent in New York City who'd expressed interest in working with me, Mike Lyons. But I couldn't just email him. I knew I would need to send him recent photos of myself and what better time to take those than a few weeks removed from the bodybuilding show. I wasn't too lean like I was on the day of the show, but I had kept myself from going overboard on eating anything after the show that would affect my health. I asked one of my friends who consider himself an amateur photographer, and a pretty damned good one if he would take a few photos of me I could send to Mike. He did.

After mailing the photos I waited patiently for an email from Mike, but several days passed and I got nothing. Then finally, four days later than expected, Mike reached out to me, and it wasn't by email. He called me directly. "Danny, I just got back into town, and I'm looking at your photos right now," he said.

Hearing his voice alone had me feeling pretty good. "Yeah?" I said.

"So, let's bring you out for a week. We'll set you up with a couple of casting calls, see what's what and go from there. How's that sound?"

"Sounds great, Mike." I was thrilled. Then I had a thought. "One more thing, Mike. I'd like to meet with a couple of acting schools. Could you set that up for me?"

"I surely can." And that was it. I took time off work and booked a roundtrip ticket.

When I arrived in Manhattan, my entire week had already been planned. Mike had me going to see the art directors of *Cosmopolitan*, *Men's Fitness*, and *Men's Health* magazines. Walking through the doors of publications I had been reading for years was an unreal feeling. I was also set up to shoot with a few photographers as well, my first professional photoshoots, to build out my portfolio. But what made me nervous was the prospect of my appointments with the acting schools, which included the New York Film Academy and the William Esper Studio. I had no clue where I wanted to go to study or how I was going to choose. The decision was going to have to be the result of a gut feeling. But as it turned out, the universe chose for me.

Later in the week, a few days after getting a private tour of the New York Film Academy and already feeling excited at the idea of going to this prestigious school, I went for my second interview at the William Esper Studio. I had no idea at that moment that I was about to meet with a legendary master teacher.

I was sitting patiently in the hallways for my interview, looking at framed photos of incredible actors from TV shows and movies that I had watched, some who were Broadway and soap opera stars. When I was instructed that it was my turn and I could make my way into the office, I stepped inside the door completely unaware of whom I would meet with. There he was, sitting in his swivel chair, wearing a button-up wool sweater over an open-collar shirt, with his salt-and-pepper hair and thick glasses.

A few things about Bill Esper: He studied directly with Sandy Meisner, creator of the acclaimed Meisner Technique, spending seventeen years as Sandy's apprentice when he was at his peak and then, for another forty years afterward dedicating his life to characterizing and continuing Sandy's work. I was a little intimidated but felt immediately more at ease once we started talking.

We chatted for about thirty minutes, discussing what the summer intensive was going to require of me and the kind of classes that were involved. It turned out to be one of the most genuine conversations I have ever had. In the end, it all came down to one deceivingly simple question: "Why are you here, Danny? I don't mean in New York City. Why are you here, today, in my office? Why do you want to study here?"

It wasn't a simple question because I'd never thought about the answer to it before that moment. The truth is that my dream had always been to act in the movies. In my imagination, I was always the actor playing the character. It was an escape fantasy. But here, I wasn't an actor; I was a student learning to be an actor, learning to play characters. It was a reality.

I knew this was the real question—the one that mattered. Over the years, Bill had probably met with hundreds of aspiring students who dreamed of studying at his studio, and asked each one of them: "Why here?" I didn't plan on how I would describe my reasons for pursuing this new aspiration, nor did I even know it when I had asked Mike to set me up to meet with these schools; I just knew it would be an important part of my journey.

"Well, Bill . . ." I took a moment to let the question sit with me and feel the truth of it. "I have wanted to be an actor ever since I can remember," I started. "Like this tall," I said, measuring my hand four feet off the ground.

"I had a few leads in my school plays, bit parts on kids shows here and there—things like that. I was in love with the world of film. I imitated my favorite actors and their performances—you know, actors I idolized growing up, like Robert De Niro in *Raging Bull* and *Taxi Driver*, Al Pacino in *The Godfather*, Brad Pitt in *Twelve Monkeys*. If you'd asked me in high school why I wanted to be an actor, my answer would have been in line with it being an escape from reality. I'd have said it made me feel alive."

"That's not the case anymore?" Bill asked.

"I still feel alive, don't get me wrong. I love it, but . . ."

First, I told Bill a little about myself, starting with the story of my father having cancer. I told him that seeing my father fight to become a better man and stay positive had changed my perspective of the man who left me when I was a kid.

Then I told him about the fitness competition I had won and how my approach to it compared to my approach to the first one. I said, "The first time I competed, I did it because I thought it would be cool. You know, with the girls. I did it to impress my friends. I didn't quite grasp the totality of work involved. My attitude showed in the results I got.

"This recent competition was different. I knew what was involved, the process of pain I would endure, the level of hard work and sacrifice required. It didn't feel cool. Not one bit. It felt daunting, and at times I wanted to quit. I was full of self-doubt. I was questioning myself every second and trying to come up with every reason to quit; and I had reasons, Bill. I came up with so many of them. But I had one reason not to. And that one reason was the only reason I needed to keep going.

"What I learned from both situations is that life is hard. It's not supposed to be easy. It's supposed to feel like you're being kicked in the head over and over again. And when you want something, I mean really want something, something worth pursuing, whether this is to live or to take yourself beyond your physical and mental limitations, you have to understand there will be struggle and obstacles. And it will always come down to your mindset.

"I can't imagine that being an actor is easy—a good one, I mean. I think it's as hard as anything, which is why there are more bad actors than good ones. And it requires a level of human spirit to become that good."

I paused momentarily. I knew there was something else. Then I continued, "It's not just being here in this office with you, Bill, that matters to me. But being here in New York City, in another city, another country, where great actors come and train, away from my friends and family, stepping completely out of the box, ready to turn my entire life upside down. I want to do this not because it's cool. It's the work I value. I know there will be sacrifices and that the experience will be daunting at times, and I may question myself. Or I may not. I don't know. But I'm here to experience it all, the journey of what it takes to be my absolute best. I learned that the journey of it all is everything; it's what matters.

"It's easy to dream about being an actor. Everybody dreams. But doing good work—that's when you know you're really chasing your dream."

Bill sat back into his chair for a moment. He looked at me and didn't say a word. I had no idea what he was thinking.

Was that the answer he wanted to hear? Or was it all hogwash? Had I been exposed as a fraud or an idiot? It felt like the longest five seconds of my life—or a close second to waiting with my breath held to hear the announcer call out the winners at the bodybuilding show. The anticipation was killing me.

He still hadn't said anything. He turned his chair toward his desk and opened up a folder in front of him. He jotted down a few notes.

I dared not speak.

As Bill continued writing in his folder, words finally came out of his mouth. "I'm going to go ahead and add you to my class, Danny."

I was not expecting Bill to say that.

I suddenly remembered that the New York Film Academy had also accepted me on the spot. As much as I wanted to say yes, I'd told them I had to respect my interview with the other school and that I would make my decision in the next day or two. They had understood. This time the acceptance felt right. The magnitude of it took my breath away for a second.

You didn't exactly tell Bill Esper, after he invited you to study the craft of acting with him, that you were still deciding. It felt as if I was Alexander the Great being invited to study with Aristotle. Not that I'm calling myself Alexander, but truly, I couldn't have been happier.

"I don't know what to say. I'm honored, Bill."

He shook my hand and told me he would be seeing me in a few months, but not before I did some homework. "Read

Sanford Meisner's book on acting before class starts. Don't forget," he instructed.

My week in New York came to an end with an offer to sign an exclusive contract with one of the top fitness modeling agencies in the city and acceptance into one of the most prestigious acting schools in the United States. It seemed bittersweet when I hopped back on the bus to the airport to return to Montreal. I knew I wasn't going back home to stay. I would be returning to New York City in a few months to pursue the dream to act that had been beating in my heart since I could remember.

I went home, quit my job, said all my goodbyes, fixed my banking information, sold my car and everything else I could, and spent as much quality time with my mom and friends as possible. Then I picked a date. On June 4, 2004, I embarked on a new adventure. I had a one-way Greyhound Bus ticket in my pocket and my entire life packed into one suitcase. I remember catching my first glimpse of the Manhattan skyline; a powerful feeling came over me: *Home!* It was just a deep sense of emotion.

This thought was followed by another little, more scared thought: *I can't believe I'm doing this.* I felt a lot of excitement and sheer joy at that moment.

We connect with each other deeper through conversation. It allows us to see ourselves through other's experiences. It blows my mind to think about how impactful one simple conversation with someone can be in an individual's life. I don't take this power for granted and realize that conversation truly is one of life's hidden treasures. Next time you speak with someone, remember that nothing in life is random. This connection is happening for a reason. There may be a lesson underway. You never know what insightful words you will hear that move you in the right direction, toward your dreams, especially when you have big dreams to chase.

At some point, you had to take responsibility for becoming the person you wanted to be and for everything that you knew. We all go through a maturation. In this process, you take all the incredible lessons you have learned, which have conditioned your behavior, you take all the wisdom from your mentors you have used to guide you, and you begin to rewire yourself through these skills you have as a human being. That's when you can begin to be your own mentor.

Remember what happened when we started making giant leaps forward because our reality changed? We needed to stop asking for permission. We started accepting more responsibility. We looked within and discovered our whys. It was all we needed. The answer to everything we seek is always in us. We were taught lessons about what motivates us and that human spirit inside each one of us, human connection and getting what we focus on, lessons only, beginnings, a framework which to build upon if understood correctly, and in this reality, we are committing to our growth.

Through experiencing life, we become a new us. We can mentor ourselves through the process of being vulnerable, following our intuition, trusting the signs of opportunity, creating a vision, and cultivating the right frame of mind, but it is the idea of the person we want to be that challenges us the most. We may not yet be everything we think we are.

We need to create a structure so we may chase a vision. Before that vision manifests, there are tests. Along the way, we must master all the lessons and create a new narrative about who we are and the capabilities we possess.

PART II

LEARNING YOUR WAY IN THE WORLD

FIVE

NEVER OVERRIDE YOUR INTUITION

Do you trust your gut?

My first month living in New York was not an easy transition. The house that my agency used to house models was full, so I had to settle for sleeping on the floor of one of the agency's apartments in Harlem. Picture the inhabitants: We were four guys. One lucky guy pulled the short straw and got the couch. The other three lay on opposite sides of the floor in the living room with our feet in one another's faces. Not quite what I was expecting for my first experience living away from home. We all knew this situation was temporary, that it gave us time to find the right place, a place whose rent we could all afford.

My days filled up fast with auditions and casting calls, photo shoots, catering work, and of course, a few hours a day in the gym—going to the gym was paramount—all while trying to see as many apartments as I could. My full-time summer intensive program at the acting studio was less than two weeks away. I knew I would need to establish a more structured routine once I started having three to four classes a day and doing homework.

It was important that I found a permanent place to live before the first day of class. I committed to renting a place with two of the other models. I felt pressed for time, but none of us wanted to rush and make the wrong decision. Between all the crazy appointments and work we got through the agency—and there was plenty in Manhattan—we squeezed in an hour here and there to check out different spots, but these were too expensive, or the smell was too questionable. Nothing felt right.

With so many students, actors, and all the young and hungry dogs on Wall Street in Manhattan looking for roommates, I suspected I'd have better luck if I looked for my own place. However, I committed myself to the other guys. Also, I liked them. I decided I just had to be patient.

Patience is an absolute must in most areas of life, and certainly when everything you are experiencing is new. Learning is a process whether you are learning about your abilities, learning to understand your surroundings, or learning how to operate in the world to get your needs met and where the dangers lie.

The Price of Ignorance: A Cautionary Tale

My days were long, and everything had to be squeezed into them, leaving me not much free time. I still was without a place to live and my classes at Esper Studio were about to begin. Searching for an apartment became more daunting. I was hoping that once I got that chore out of the way, I could start to embrace the experience of living in New York fully.

One evening, I returned to the apartment in Harlem and discovered that someone had tried to break in. The doorknob was kicked in. I found my agent and one of the other models giving statements to a police officer. Very quickly, panic set in as I realized I had an envelope stashed in my suitcase that contained about $5,000 in cash from my savings to get me started. Never did it cross my mind that it wouldn't be safe if left in the suitcase. Not even for a second. This was for rent, gym membership, and day-to-day things I needed, like food. Of course. I couldn't believe it. *My first month in New York City, and I get robbed? Are you fucking kidding me?! Already, I've become a cautionary tale.*

I ran to my bag, still exactly where I'd left it in the corner of the living room. It was still zipped up. I opened it and found the envelope. The cash was still there—massive sigh of relief. As I said, being robbed never crossed my mind before then.

But the incident didn't make any sense. Oddly, nothing had been stolen. The other models had everything they brought with them, and nothing was taken from the agent's house either. The only evidence present of foul play was that the front door had been kicked in.

Was the burglar scared away? How do we even explain the door getting kicked in? There were many unanswered quest-ions. The four of us guys knew we needed to find a new place to live in a hurry. Three of us decided to move in together.

That very night I happened to get a reply on Craigslist about a studio apartment available for rent on the Upper West Side. *Please, God, let this place be the one,* I thought. My cohorts and I rode the C Train downtown to West 86th Street and Central Park West. The moment we stepped out of the subway exit and onto the sidewalk, we were facing Central Park. It was a remarkable sight to see. I hadn't even seen the place yet, and I wanted to live there, near the park.

We made our way down the block toward Columbus Avenue and couldn't help noticing how beautifully structured each building was, with the majority of buildings having a doorman. All I could think about was getting the hell out of our current situation. In comparison, this place looked like heaven.

The address we had took us to the corner of 86th and Columbus Avenue, to a beautiful brownstone building, five stories high and, conveniently, within a few blocks distance of everything you could possibly want. You could get to Crunch Gym by going one way, Equinox and the New York Sports Club by going three blocks the other way, and a shit ton of restaurants, bars, and supermarkets. I had never seen so many stores clumped up into one single area. Not to mention quick, easy access to the subway both on Central

Park West and on Broadway two blocks the other way. I was sold on the location, and I hadn't seen the place yet.

My thoughts were: *Unless this place turns out to be a total shit hole, I am ready to give the landlord a down payment right here and now, this very night.*

We buzzed in and looked at apartment 1A. I was already in love with the idea of living in the building. And this is where my cautionary tale must start. The name of the guy we met was Brian. He was a former model from the '90s whose big claim to fame was that he had appeared in a music video for one of the greatest rock bands in music history. We took a tour of the place, which was basically us turning in a complete 360-degree circle in the middle of the living room. It had a second-floor loft bed taking up half the ceiling space, but a nice corner space underneath the stairs that could fit an airbag, and one comfortable couch. I started figuring out how we would be able to fit each one of us into our own space inside the apartment. It was doable. So, we started talking terms. The rent was just south of $3,000 a month.

I didn't know anything about New York City rental prices and what was acceptable. I just assumed that this amount for a studio on the Upper West Side in a beautiful brownstone building a block away from Central Park made sense; plus, divided between three guys, it didn't seem so bad.

And this is when I should have realized something was off. I was about to be offered a lesson about the difference between gut instincts and ignorance. But how well I would learn it would depend on how well I was paying attention.

Gut Feeling #1

"Guys, I have to let you know, I have two girls who are interested in this place," Brian said. "In fact, they're ready to put down a two-month deposit right now. But I like you guys—you said you're three guys. I feel I can trust you guys,"

Here's the thing, I knew that line was bullshit. It was just a feeling I had almost instantly even before my brain could decipher it. And it did: If he'd had two girls ready to give him $6,000, he would have taken it. So, either the girls didn't exist, or perhaps they did and saw the place and told him they thought it was too expensive. Despite the uneasy gut feeling I was getting and knowing it was bullshit, I wanted the place badly. I wanted to put the entire ordeal of a messy burglary behind me and get out of that other apartment so that I could start focusing on my acting classes.

Remember, I said I had to learn to be more patient. I was impatient, and so were my buddies. Brian's words pushed us to take action. We all agreed on it and arranged to meet him the next day and bring him the first and the last months' rent as a deposit.

Result: I chose to perpetuate my ignorance because I wanted the place. *What's the worst that could happen.?* I thought.

Gut Feeling #2

The next day my friends and I met Brian with an envelope stacked with hundreds. I had the envelope in my hand, and before I handed it over, he had one more thing to add: "Just one thing," he started to say. "If you happen to see a blond woman walking around, just ignore her."

Okay, the first lie had seemed harmless enough, as many real estate agents exaggerate the truth to push a sale or rental, but now I was getting that uneasy gut feeling with an unwavering suspicion. I was handing over all this money to this guy. "If she asks who you are, tell her you're my cousins."

Warning flags on high alert. *Why would a blond woman ask us who we are?* There was a moment of silence after Brian told us that. We all looked at each other. But then he quickly made his escape. "Here are the keys. You have my number. If you need to get a hold of me, call me any time." He left.

A few days later, I got home from my first week at the studio. Halfway up the stoop of the building, I walked past a blond woman heading out the door. She seemed lovely enough and wished me a nice day. I noticed her turn and look back at me while making her way to the corner of the block while I was using the front door key.

My roommates had their own experiences of passing the same woman coming home. They all said the same thing: that she was nice and didn't cause any issues or ask any questions.

The second week, I was going through a solid everyday routine: waking up early, going to classes, and hitting the gym between them, going to casting calls. One particular day, in the afternoon, I had passed the front door, and just as I was turning the key to the door of the apartment, I heard footsteps coming down the stairs. "Excuse me," a voice from behind me said. "Who are you?"

It was that very same blond woman we were told to ignore. I was startled. I didn't want to lie. I wanted to tell her who I was, but I kept thinking about what Brian told us, and I didn't. I had that suspicious gut feeling again. "I'm Brian's cousin," I answered. That felt wrong on so many levels.

"Okay, great," she said. "Well, will you do me a favor? Please tell your cousin he needs to call me. I've been trying to reach him for a few weeks now, and he hasn't called me back."

Result: I chose to perpetuate my ignorance. *Hopefully, this will blow over*, I thought.

Gut Feeling #3

I called Brian. No answer. Sent him a few texts. No answer. A few days went by. No word from Brian. And all three of us started having more quick run-ins with the woman.

One morning, pretty early on a Sunday, there was a knock at the door. Nobody moved. And then another knock. Nothing. "Hello." On the other side of the door was the blond woman. I recognized her voice. We all did. We started getting up slowly. This woman wasn't going anywhere. Okay, it was time to face the music and figure out what was going on. We were all up.

"So, what's the deal guys? Who are you, and where is Brian?" She did not sound quite like the same sweet woman we had encountered before. You could see it in her face and hear it in her voice: She wasn't happy and felt extremely frustrated.

"Brian rented us the place a few weeks ago. We've been trying to get a hold of him, but he's since disappeared," we told her.

"Isn't that interesting?" she replied. "Because I rented him this place four weeks ago and he owes me rent money."

Result: Screwed. *I should have seen this coming,* I thought. But I did see this coming.

There it was. The truth. The blond woman was the landlord. She owned the building. That wasn't even the worst part. There was more. "How much did you guys pay him for rent?" If it was even possible for that feeling in my stomach to get even more uneasy, there it was. "Rent for this place is actually $2,100 a month. Looks like we all got swindled."

We'd just been ripped off. An ironic twist, considering I'd thought I had been robbed of all my money a few weeks before. No warning signs there. This time around was a different story.

I couldn't believe that pretending to be a landlord was a thing. Somebody went out of his way to rent this place, only to re-rent it again to someone else for a thousand extra, plus a security deposit, and take off. I couldn't help but think; *There has to be a special place in hell for somebody like this.*

Long story short, the woman was extremely sympathetic about our situation and let us stay for the remainder of the first month without paying more. We started paying her directly after that.

Is our gut feeling important to a spontaneous life?

There is no spontaneous life if you don't trust that gut feeling. Your intuition begins and ends with trusting yourself. For most people, that's a lot to ask.

You might be thinking you don't even know what that looks like or how that feels. But you do.

Your mind tells you something. You believe it to be true. Because it looks so perfect. And you don't want anything to take that away from you. End of story. That's not how your intuition works.

Your intuition goes beyond basic analytical thinking. It's a feeling created by your ability to understand what's happening without being consciously aware of it. It's that hunch you get.

You were born with instincts. It is human coded in every one of us. As kids, we acted with impulse. Everything was a biological response. It was just so easy to follow. If your instinct was to start laughing, you didn't think about it, you just laughed. And if it was to cry, you pretty much didn't give a shit about crying. Your first reaction was usually the one you went with.

Intuition is the first moment of truth. Now, because you are older, it may feel easier to go the other way; but you can also ride that moment and be completely spontaneous.

Of course, being a child is very different from being an adult. As adults, we have the ability to process the messages of our intuition because as the mind sharpens itself with age and experience, so does the intuition. The sum of every instinct, insight, or hunch you ever had drives your intuition to be as accurate as it generally is in sniffing out lies and danger.

All men and women who have ever done something great in their own lives or contributed to the lives of others have been able to do so in large measure because of intuition. It's important to understand that instinct is not a feeling. It's an automatic reaction hardwired in us that is triggered by the environment, a framework upon which we build both intuition and logic. Your intuition allows you to see the truth without the certainty of facts and logic. It sees what's in front of you without the filter of bias. It is so important to trust in your intuition because it never takes sides. It's all about truth. The gut feelings you have will always tell you what's up, whereas the nonsensical voice in your head will always tell you what you want to hear—and try to match the facts to your belief system.

When you're young, it's easy to mistake what you think is right with what you want or hope to be right. Part of learning to survive on your own is learning to trust yourself when making decisions and remember that your immediate feeling most often is the correct one. That reaction is spontaneous, connected with the present moment—every single time.

If you don't make a point of listening to the wisdom of your gut, it won't take long for the mind to jump in and start telling you the stories and offering up the justifications you want to hear to find a reason to do what you want that is in opposition to your intuition. And most times, that overriding happens in mere seconds—by which time, you're screwed.

Trust your instincts. Trust your intuition. Trust yourself.

SIX

A MASTER CLASS IN VULNERABILITY

Can you let go and give in?

Each of us is conditioned to be a certain way as a child. As a result of osmosis and direct instruction, by the time we are able to reason we have internalized rules for our behavior that keep us from being free and emotionally vulnerable. In my case, I learned rules such as: be strong, not weak; think before you speak; keep your emotions to yourself. To be a decent actor, I needed to be deconditioned.

It has been quite some time since I sat in that classroom writing down every bit of wisdom Bill Esper shared with us in my notebook. Periodically I love to troll through these scribbled down points of reference, which I can barely read anymore, and I continue to find them relevant to my life.

When I first stepped through the door of the William Esper Studio on West 42nd Street in Manhattan on June 15, 2004, I began an incredible life-changing journey as a student of the craft of acting. Two and a half years later, when I stepped out of that building for the last time as a student, not only was I a graduate of the two-year-long acting program, and a trained, skilled actor, I was also further along the path to mastering something that would take me beyond acting, my emotions. Vulnerability is fundamental to creating a spontaneous life. Acting was no longer an escape from reality that I used to feel alive and fully immersed in the present. Now I felt alive and fully immersed in every moment. Acting was my profession.

Back on that clear spring day in 2004, my commitment was only to join the summer intensive. Of course, I had no idea at the time that I signed up for the ultimate master class in human experience. The desire for the ongoing evolution of self that was reinforced by participating in this course of study would become my driving force for the rest of my life so far.

There was nothing quite like that first day. From the moment I woke up, I was ready to go "full Daniel Day-Lewis" on my craft. Seating myself in that studio for the first time, where strangers surrounded me in chairs situated on low risers, facing the southern end of the space—the stage—was exhilarating. We did not know that before long, we would become the closest people in each other's lives for the next two years. Watching each other grow into a level of vulnerability was more transformational than any of us has ever suspected it would be.

In that time, through the various exercises and guidance given to us, we shared experience. We began working with partners, notably from two equally important classes: acting class and movement class. I let go of trying to be who I thought I was supposed to be and started building the skills that would support me in being the person I was. With those skills, I was able to engage wholeheartedly in my first live performance as the principal male lead in my first and only Off-Broadway theatrical performance. Developing these skills together as a class was as beautiful to watch as it was to feel and experience, and it all started on day one when Bill walked into our class and told us about a little Martian that visited Earth.

Stay with me. The story gets better.

But first, let's put this into perspective. I am no longer a working actor or working toward becoming one. Nonetheless, my time at the Studio has been invaluable in every conceivable area of my life from my physical and mental state and emotional strength, and my professional life, to my relationships with friends, family, colleagues, significant others, and self. It has helped me to follow my spiritual path toward fulfillment. I can't say it enough. I truly feel I would not be the person I am today—the man writing this book—if I hadn't gone through the experiences that I did in the acting studio which I am now about to share with you.

Also, I don't expect that you are an actor or that you are working toward being one. The reason I am sharing my stories is because of the value of the lessons to the pursuit of being human—and especially of being a vulnerable human who is attempting to live spontaneously.

So, let's begin your masterclass in vulnerability.

"Suppose you're walking down the street," Bill Esper said, "and you have a run-in with a little, four-foot-tall green alien. Not somebody in a costume. The real deal. A real, living, breathing alien. Short build, green skin, and two antennae sticking out the top of its head. An actual alien from another planet. So, you strike up a conversation—you know, a little chit chat. He asks what you're holding. You say, "It's a latte from Starbucks." You ask, 'Are there any Starbucks on Mars?' That sort of a thing.

"Then the Martian asks you, 'What is it you do?'

"You say, 'I'm an actor.' But the Martian has no idea what an actor is. They have no such professions on Mars. So, how would you explain to this little green alien, what an actor is exactly?"

The class didn't say a word. Everybody was hesitant until one hand went up, then others followed. I heard "performer," "entertainer," then I raised my hand. "Storyteller," I said.

After a few more responses, Bill gave us his working definition. "Acting is the ability to live truthfully under imaginary circumstances."

He then broke down the definition into two important factors. The first factor is to live truthfully. This would be the core of our work as actors—acting's lifeblood. Bill said, "Actors are fantastic liars because those lies are always grounded in truth and serve the purpose of their art."

The second factor is the ability to use your truth under imaginary circumstances. The ability to imagine is the pivotal skill for an actor to develop. I would also say that imagination is the greatest source of potential for all human beings as its scope is limitless.

A man with one of the greatest minds in history, theoretical physicist Albert Einstein, said, "Imagination is more important than knowledge. For knowledge is limited, whereas imagination embraces the entire world, stimulating progress, giving birth to evolution."[1]

Last I checked, Einstein wasn't an actor. But it was imagining the possibilities of what the universe could be that led him to develop the theory of relativity. The knowledge he acquired while running through all sorts of mathematical possibilities related to relativity was based on the idea that one equation eventually would be discovered that can explain all the beautiful mysteries of the universe.

Little known fact: Einstein's work was based on what he called *thought experiments*, otherwise known as daydreams. Einstein's imagination was the engine that drove him to produce his life's work, a lasting legacy that changed our world.

With the idea of living truthfully under imaginary circumstances, our class had a working definition to describe what we did for a living if ever the need arose to explain it to someone, even a Martian. Be warned.

Becoming a Student of Vulnerability

"Seeds are extremely important. It is the very core of where we start to build the skills to become a great actor. Everything starts with a proper beginning. That beginning is called Repetition," Bill said.[2]

Repetition was the foundational technique in the first series of training exercises Bill gave us to develop our skills as actors. This technique would be used specifically to develop and enhance our impulses. Through this teaching, we would be learning that everything we do and say in life comes from how we see the world subjectively. We have to learn to trust our impulses. This truth will influence the actor's imagination.

I immediately recognized the difficulty of the exercise for me: As a child, I had been taught never to behave impulsively. I grew up with the idea that everything should be considered fully and in the most logical way before reacting. That's what my teachers told me. That's what my mom told me. That was what I knew to do.

Being taught to restrain your impulses is like being four years old and getting your hand slapped if you reach for a cookie on the table before dinner. If you get your hand slapped enough times, then you stop reaching out.

Now I was being told to take the cookie off the damned table.

This would be challenging.

I raised my hand. "Bill, why is impulse important? I was always taught otherwise."

"Of course, you were, Danny," Bill said, before addressing my question. "Repetition has everything to do with the reality of *really doing* because it forces you to *really listen* and *really answer* whatever you hear. That is the seed that I so often speak of, from which all good acting develops."

So, to explain the exercise in a vacuum, whatever your acting partner says, you repeat it back. Eventually, someone is going to have an organic impulse to change the flow of the exchange. At which point that person just follows their impulse.

In pairs, we stood in front of the class and worked on repetition. I looked at my partner, deciding how to start. She was wearing a beat-up looking hat. "Your hat looks beat up," I said.

"My hat looks beat up," she repeated.

"Yeah, your hat looks beat up."

Again, she repeated, "Yeah, my hat looks beat up."

Then I thought (first mistake), *Let's change it up.* "Your beat-up-looking hat suits you," I said.

"No." Bill stopped me. "You can't just think your way into changing a shift. It's wrong. It's inorganic. It's calculated."

He explains this same point very clearly in his book *The Actor's Art and Craft.*

> *We don't seek to develop our* minds *with Repetition; rather we seek to develop our instincts. Everything that happens in Repetition should be driven by* impulses. *Emotions. You must respond to what you hear from your partner* without analysis. *Any time you engage your mind*

during Repetition, you'll mask your true impulses and throw yourself off the exercise.[3]

A few paragraphs later, Bill writes:

A connection with his impulses is one of the most important things an actor can develop, because who you really are is revealed by your spontaneous impulses. Not the "you" that you'd like to be or the "you" you think another person wants you to be. I'm talking about your true self.[4]

I understood completely what Bill was saying: A response to something we've heard someone say should come from the reality of really listening to that person rather than from thinking about what we want to hear or want to say next. In the Meisner Technique, the only way that Repetition can change is by responding to your partner's behavior.

But understanding it didn't make it any easier to do.

This one simple exercise, Repetition, was the basis of everything else we would explore that summer, as well as over the next two years of the full-length acting program, from the importance of doing tasks, to script work and emotional connection. All acting comes from understanding that everything done or said onstage must hold a seed of truth; without a seed of truth in our work, we would never progress.

How often do we genuinely listen to one another in life and respond to the reality of what we're hearing? Not often enough. Listening is the basis of human connection. It's a skill we all should practice so we can be more honest and vulnerable with one another.

To begin to listen more fully, you have to practice being present and paying attention. In listening attentively, you are putting your focus entirely on somebody else and thereby creating what is essentially a selfless state. It only works in the present moment. The power to truly listen with an open mind allows you to gain a new perspective and experience a shift in your reality. You gain understanding.

You won't experience true vulnerability in conversation until you begin to listen. Because when you let your guard down enough to hear what is being said and see the body language of the person speaking to you, you discover what your heart is telling you about what you're hearing and seeing. You can "hear" what your instincts are telling you.

How can we cultivate a better understanding of what stops us from listening to our hearts and walking into the complete unknown, open, vulnerable, and spontaneously? By building the skills to listen and follow our instincts. By removing the layers of defense. By deciding to take one more step into vulnerability.

Movement Is an Avenue to Emotional Vulnerability and Human Connection

In one of my top ten favorite books ever, *Daring Greatly*, author Brené Brown writes: "We are hardwired to connect with others, it's what gives purpose and meaning to our lives, and without it, there is suffering."[5]

Welcome to Movement Class, stressing physical freedom and emotional openness and release. A class where I would find connection. The purpose of the work done here was initially to pinpoint and dissolve physical blocks in the body that were inhibiting our ability to process our ongoing experience freely. It would then progress to alignment and physical characterization. To do the work properly, we had to give up our focus on trying to be cool and begin the process of letting go.

The principles we would learn in this class would become tremendously important for the sake of our growth. Through practices that included different forms of dance and creating laughter, we would learn to create stillness and tranquility to release the anxiety that fundamentally runs many people's lives. The essential elements in them all were letting go of what people think of you and of always trying to be in control.

No wonder this was my least favorite class. I had always tried to be in control and, like billions more people, I cared what people thought about me. That meant the class might be tougher than Bill's class.

We began every class the same way: lying on the ground on our backs in complete silence for ten minutes. Not a word. Not a single movement. Lights turned off. We were just to come in and immediately grab a spot on the floor, settling into Corpse pose (in Sanskrit, *Savasana)*, with our arms and legs spread just a bit and our palms facing upward. After ten minutes of stillness, our teacher, Ted, would begin the class by playing music to get us moving and awaken our bodies.

The point of this preliminary exercise was to clear our minds of any thoughts, focus on breathing deeply, and allow ourselves to experience simply being there in that studio sharing the moment with everybody else. Ted would put on music—he was partial to "Svefn-G-Englar" by Sigur Ros and "Nothing Compares" by Sinéad O'Connor—and when we got an impulse to move with the music, we would slowly and patiently take our time getting up off the floor and onto our feet, keeping our eyes closed.

You might hear an occasional "Oops" when hands accidentally touched, but that was okay. The point was just to go with it and not think. To move and free yourself of any fears of judgment and rejection.

If we touched, maybe our hands would start moving together in one direction, and maybe they would eventually part ways. One day you might stay a little longer on the floor. Maybe something emotional was happening inside you, and you needed to release it.

The music was always different. Sometimes it started slowly, but it always ended with everybody high kicking and having a good time. Do you know the adage "Dance like nobody is watching"? Well, that's exactly what movement class was like. Nobody was watching, and nobody cared.

Dancing without inhibition did not come easy to me at first—and that's a big overstatement.

I never meditated in my life before I stepped foot in acting school. It wasn't a thing anyone ever told me about. Lying on the floor and breathing was a strange experience. I can tell you I had a hundred thoughts per minute running through my head during that first class, and during the next and the one after that. Also, I can tell you that my hand moved away quickly and suddenly any time I accidentally touched someone else. So yeah, I didn't like the class.

And then I loved it. Because the moment I let go of my fear of judgment and my fear of rejection, I experienced something completely different and new. It was freedom, it was liberation, it was stepping away from my thoughts and staying completely present in my body.

This release happened after a few weeks. On the day it did, I never got off the ground. I couldn't breathe. It was as if every breath was being pulled out of my lungs. Seeing this, Ted came near me and told me to let go. So, I did. I cried.

I cried at that moment for reasons I never knew, and I have never tried to find any logical rationale for it. Maybe I was tired of my fears. Maybe I was tired of feeling so much pain stuck inside me. All I know is that at that moment, I experienced a level of vulnerability that I can only describe as powerful beyond belief—a state of vulnerability that became instrumental to my acting as well as my primary way of being.

We tend to carry so much stress in our bodies that we begin to restrict ourselves of the body's abilities to connect without fear. This unwanted negative energy weighs us down emotionally and physically. In allowing our bodies to start releasing through this kind of work, through utilizing our natural hardwiring for connection, we are freeing unwanted energy and creating room in our bodies for emptiness and presence.

We hear it too often. Life is short and unpredictable. That's perhaps why there's so much power in movement—and the world needs plenty of it.

Dancing dissolves physical limitations in the body. Close your eyes and dance at home every night like you are the greatest dancer in the world. As if you've been discovered on TikTok and millions are watching you. Dance honestly, doing whatever you need to do to start getting comfortable in your own body. Build your freedom of movement, and you'll begin to create awareness of your power and freedom in your consciousness.

Movement dissolves physical limitations in the body and enables us to go deeper with ourselves and each other. This is another step towards embracing vulnerability, another step in creating a spontaneous life. The importance of physical synergy and interaction in dance and of expressing the silliness that your body can express if you approach dancing without judgment cannot be understated. Dancing with other people is a means of allowing yourself to experience connection and vulnerability fully.

Vulnerability Is an Act of Courage

It was in the middle of our second year of Meisner training when my friend Nico rushed home suddenly one day because his father died. He had such a close bond with his father that they were like brothers. His dad was the CEO of a major company, and he had learned everything required of a man from his father, including leadership skills. In February of that year, Nico's father was diagnosed with aggressive colon cancer. It was late October when he passed away.

Nico and I weren't in the same acting class, but we studied movement together, and I was closer to him than to my classmates in scene study. We shared words many times and had become friends. He was gone a week. His first day back after his father's death was difficult for him. Having lost my dad to cancer, his experience resonated with me. I can recall how much I had Nico in my heart and on my mind. So did our classmates.

We started movement class as we usually did, lying on the ground in complete silence. Ten minutes went by, and then Ted played the music signifying it was time to dance around the room with our eyes closed. Everybody took their time getting themselves fully on both feet. Slowly we rolled to our sides, then turned and placed one knee on the ground, while the other leg sat across it. And then the other stood next to it. This day was different. As each of us made our way to our feet, we felt ourselves pull into each other, forming a circle with Nico in the center. There was no fear of touching that day. We all let go completely and fully. It just felt right. I could hear Nico crying, and we were all there with him. He didn't hold back.

Nico told me, "I knew that movement class was going to be very powerful for me. Lying on that floor for the first five minutes, I let down my guard. I felt overwhelmed and yet . . . like this was a safe place. My emotions were overflowing, so

I just started uncontrollably crying and let them out." He allowed himself to be vulnerable, and we supported him as he dropped his defenses. We are connected to him each moment, and we were connected to ourselves.

In his book *Shift into Freedom*, psychologist and meditation teacher Loch Kelly explains:

> *When we experience a great loss or hurt that feels like 'brokenheartedness,' we now realize that our heart is not broken. It's actually the heart's protective shell of defenses breaking open to allow us to feel all emotions fully.*[6]

I have concluded that vulnerability is an act of courage. During vulnerable moments, we unite with our authentic self, instead of hiding it behind a battleground of repression.

Nico and I talked years later about that experience. "I felt selfish. I was in a classroom with so many other people and, I felt a little guilty at first, but then I said forget it and just gave in. We changed the whole structure of the class that day. I didn't realize it at the time, but I could see the impact the experience had on other people as well. I think it broke through a lot of layers of defense for other people too. I remember going around and hugging everyone, and it helped me realize more and more how I loved my father so much and how strong a capacity for love I have in me.

"It was such a strong cry, one of the strongest cries of my life, that at the end of the class I was exhausted because I had released so many feelings that had been bottled up inside of me. You're never the same person after going through a catharsis like that."

I have always felt that for myself and the rest of the students what transpired that day was about leaning into the reality of the experience, and connecting to one another with openness and compassion. In loosening my defenses, I was taught that I could trust and rely on my friends when I was in a tight spot—that a natural empathy emerges when we are authentic.

Vulnerability Is an Avenue to Human Connection

In the second year of actor training, an opportunity came up for me to work with an aspiring Latin American actress from the Esper Studio. Luciana was looking for a leading man for an original, three-character play that was about sixty pages (and minutes) long. She was to play the female lead in the show, which she was producing as a means of showcasing her talents for agents, producers, and friends.

Luciana had booked a theater on West 47th Street just off Broadway and was ready to sink a lot of money into the show. She was going to have posters and postcards designed and printed. She had hired a costume designer, a prop manager, and a director. She was all in. She just needed to find the right actor for her counterpart. For me, it would be an incredible opportunity to showcase my work, as well.

We had three months to prepare for our run. Preparation included scheduled time to read together and separately with the director, as well as to do the work on the script that we put in on our own time. My role required me to speak in a Southern accent. I found a dialect coach through my school who agreed to work with me twice a week. The intensity of the experience was not unlike training for the bodybuilding competition I had won in Canada a few years earlier; it was all-consuming.

For the next three months, my life was turned upside down. I had a full-time class schedule and rehearsals with my classmates to prepare scene work for class, in addition to a few modeling jobs and workouts to do. Every second in between would be dedicated to studying my lines for the play. And did I mention, I had the task of memorizing a twelve-minute monologue in the second half that was extremely emotionally driven?

Every week the lines become more fluid. Bill was always extremely adamant with his students about the importance of preparation. He told us rehearsals outside the studio were as important to the work if not more than the time spent in class. And he often reminded us that he didn't have the patience for anyone who wasn't prepared. The lines must become second nature so you can give yourself over completely to the flow in every moment. That was what we were training for.

I took his admonitions to heart. I rehearsed those lines doing the dishes, making lunch, riding the subway every day, in the gym between weight lifting, running, rowing on a cardio machine, or walking down Broadway. No script in hand. No emotional attachment. As mechanically as possible. By the time we were down to a month left before opening night, that script was encoded in my DNA, and my voice sounded full-on Southern, like Matthew McConaughey. My roommates had forgotten what I sounded like.

This was easily the hardest work I had ever put into anything, and that includes my three-month bodybuilding show preparation when I lost nearly forty pounds. I was dedicated, employing a razor-sharp work ethic, but I wouldn't know how ready I was until opening night.

So, the big night comes. I'm sitting backstage as the auditorium fills up. My mom has flown into New York City to see me, my entire class and my friends show up, as do casting directors and agents, and what seems like hundreds more people. My nerves also show up, and they're feasting in my gut. Performing in front of twenty of my peers in class was one thing; it was another thing doing it in front of an audience of 200.

The curtains open. The second female lead delivers an incredible opening monologue. She plays a nun sheltered in her room in the convent. I'm waiting patiently at the stage exit for my cue. The first act goes great—just like we rehearsed it for so many months. All the right cues are hit. We connect in every scene. My nerves are frayed no more.

It's intermission now, and I know my big monologue is coming in the second half. I am feeling much more confident. Eager to get back onstage.

At the top of the second act, Luciana is on stage alone. Fully immersed in her character, she starts reminiscing about the night her husband was killed. She is an absolute joy to watch. And now my big moment arrives. On stage in front of that many people, twelve minutes can seem an eternity. I come out wearing an old, torn-up Civil War uniform, shirt riddled with bullet holes, and blood stains running down to my shoes. I am playing the ghost of her husband speaking to her. She cannot see me.

I am dragging my prop gun on the floor behind me as I walk toward centerstage where I stop and gaze upon her. With my Southern dialect, I begin my monologue. I walk over and kneel close to my wife. I feel exposed, vulnerable, and yet fearless. I look at her for a moment and repeat every single line that is imprinted on my brain successfully. I am just giving myself to the moment fluidly.

Then, suddenly, the strangest thing happens. I look away momentarily into the crowd. It is no more than a split-second shift in focus. At that moment, I could see the faces of my classmates staring at me despite the glare of the spotlight. So much can happen in a split-second. I am disconnected from my train of thought, and the next line has vanished. Quite possibly, the worst thing that could have happened to me does happen. I freeze. I am completely blank.

Well, not exactly.

My mind is racing. It sounds like *Holy shit! What's my line? Holy shit. What's my line? Holy shit. What's my line? Holy shit. What's my line? Holy shit. What's my line? Holy shit! Holy shit! Holy shit! Holy shit! Holy shit! Holy shit! F*CK ME!*

My mind is running through a thousand thoughts a minute. The words in my head are getting louder. Fear set upon me almost immediately. It is the most terrifying thing I've ever experienced in my body. I don't know what to do.

This is all happening in seconds, but it feels much longer.

Luciana looks at me, realizing something is wrong.

I close my eyes for a second, take a deep breath, and in my head I hear the voice of my wise master, Bill, speaking to me, "You can place your concentration where you want it to be."

I forget about the crowd and the agents and casting directors watching. I open my eyes and solely place my focus on Luciana. Tears are in her eyes.

That was the moment when I felt completely exposed. And the vulnerability I had worked to build over the previous year now allowed me to let go of my self-doubt immediately so I could return my focus to the work, the moment, and to the truth of my connection to Luciana. The reality of her presence saved me.

Because I had planted a seed in my heart through my training and practice, I was able to give in and be there with her, fully present in the moment. Attentively listening and taking her in. That moment was when I allowed myself to become completely emotionally available to her.

My lines came back to me.

Brené Brown's research has shown us that "when we pretend that we can avoid vulnerability we engage behaviors that are often inconsistent with who we want to be. Experiencing vulnerability isn't a choice—the only choice we have is how we're going to respond when we confronted with uncertainty, risk, and emotional exposure."[7]

Doing meaningful work matters. Meaning keeps us engaged, deepens our connection to what matters, and makes us come alive and be willing to risk the vulnerability of being spontaneous.

Every performance after that evening was incredible, but we will always remember that first night. That first night was so special. We stood together, side by side, hand in hand, to a roaring standing ovation from all our peers and our friends. And in front of my mom. I was so incredibly proud. We both were. Because we knew how much work we put into these roles. Because I knew I broke barriers I had maintained for so long, and I'd freed myself so that I could play this character. I went to places I'd never been. I was vulnerable in every moment, and I discovered that was a beautiful way to be. I found strength in vulnerability. I found spontaneity there. And I felt self-realized.

I will always thank Bill Esper for the seed of this performance which he planted in me on the first day of class.

A personal favorite quote of mine, something that Bill would always tell us in class, which is written in *The Actor's Art and Craft*, is this.

> *Without vulnerability, you cannot obtain that emotional fluidity that audiences find so affecting. And you should take great comfort in the fact that, once you accept the danger contained in revealing yourself, only then can you become strong. Because there is great strength in*

accepting your willingness to experience, feel, to surrender completely to one's experience of life. The actor's mantra should, 'Give up, give in, give way.'[8]

This is the ultimate human experience. We are conditioned to survive. We have been taught that vulnerability is a weakness. In fact, it is a strength. The process of reconditioning yourself to be more connected and open will bring you up against many tests and obstacles. You will find yourself questioning why you're letting yourself reveal your emotion, particularly when the old way of being seems more comfortable.

In the process, you will become more self-aware of where and how your emotional unavailability is holding you back from deeper connections, more powerful work, self-acceptance, and self-love. You'll stop looking at vulnerability as a flaw. You will find courage and strength to give in to complete freedom of being emotionally vulnerable and emotionally available. This is where spontaneity exists.

In every hero's journey, the hero meets a wise master who mentors him. For me, on my journey of learning to live spontaneously, the wise master was Bill Esper, who helped me decondition myself from the ways I had been taught to live and think so I could tap into what is perhaps the greatest untapped human superpower: emotional vulnerability.

Remember, vulnerability is a state of being. It is a choice you make again and again to drop your guard and be connected where you are and no matter whom you are with at present. Do whatever you have to do to decondition yourself so you can be free and alive.

SEVEN

THE UNIVERSE DOESN'T MAKE SENSE

Can you go with the flow?

I'll never forget the day I was sitting all alone outside a boarding gate at JFK Airport, hours before my flight home to Canada, completely perplexed and contemplating a series of events that had unfolded during the previous year and how my plans for my future had all come crashing down on me in the past few weeks. *What just happened? Where did I go wrong? How could I not have seen this coming?*

This story, of course, involves a girl.

What was supposed to be a love story had turned into a tragedy. Not the mainstream evening news kind of tragedy, just the kind that had me scratching my head and feeling blue. Think TikTok rant gone viral. My fairy-tale romance ended as a sinister funhouse filled with smoke and mirrors.

Retrospect is powerful. Today I can tell you that amazing things happened in the aftermath of the events I am about to recount, which proves to me that nothing in our lives is random. Despite how heartbroken you feel or how much you think life sucks, every door that shuts tightly closed in front of us is an invitation to look for another door—because a bigger, better possibility is waiting for us.

Before I get to the good stuff, the really cool stuff that happened, I have to bring you back to how I ended up in that boarding area on my way home feeling perplexed and utterly crushed.

I'm not going to lie. This story about how when one door closed for me another opportunity was right there in front of me, although I couldn't see it until I started focusing on what I could control and letting of what I couldn't plays like a solid Netflix series—half comedy, half drama. I experienced great moments of inspiration when I was finally stunned to acknowledge that the universe had always had my back, that I just needed to open myself to receive.

After graduating from the acting conservatory and spending the next year or so doing odd jobs and modeling, but nothing fulfilling, I had an opportunity to work with a theater company in Toronto. I made a move to the brand-new city, which was lively and exciting, like New York, but not like New York. Unfortunately, the company was short lived. Before I could even get my feet wet, it was gone, and I found myself working in the same franchise restaurant as

I did in Montreal years earlier. I had a freshly inked signature on a one-year lease on an apartment. The only thing I didn't have was an acting job. The money was great, but it felt like I was living in some deja-vu time warp. Same restaurant, different city.

Of course, I thought about moving back to New York, but the unimaginable happened: I got comfortable. I mean, unnervingly, uncomfortably comfortable! That's the worst kind of comfort. Here I was, in my late twenties, in a city that I didn't really love because of my circumstances, away from all the friends I'd made in the prior years, with not many companions, putting away enormous amounts of cash, and yet, for the first time in my life that I could recall, I lacked any serious ambition. When I'd moved to New York in my early twenties, I was full of ambition. Now staring into the "dark abyss" of my thirties, I didn't have much of a plan.

Then I saw a glimmer of hope. Her name was Mary, and she was from San Francisco. She was the first girl I met online—through Facebook. I came across her blog via my newsfeed and thought she was engaging and sweet. I don't know what compelled me to write to her, but I did; and to tell you the truth, I don't even remember what my message said. Then she wrote back, and after exchanging a few messages, we started Skyping with each other. My Skype sessions with Mary became the highlights of my week—we chatted after work, before work, and while doing laundry on a Saturday night. I would situate my open laptop facing the ironing board as I flattened my trousers and button-down work shirts.

The thing I enjoyed about Mary was reading her blog posts, and they were blowing up. Everybody had a blog, including people's pets—well, everybody but me. I found other ways to write, such as journaling, scribbling poems in my binder when I felt artistic, and noodling around on the occasional movie script, but nothing I was ready for the world to see. And this started to get me thinking: *What's my message? What would I say if I had an audience?*

After six to eight months of Skyping a few times a week, it was fair to say that Mary and I thought we knew each other reasonably well, except for the fact that we had never actually met face to face. You know, a minor detail. So, I proposed that we meet and suggested we do this on neutral ground—in New York City, of course. My old training partner and good friend Jorge from back when New York was home said we could stay with him. Tickets were booked, bags were packed, and a fire was lit in my belly because I was returning to the city to meet my lady love. It was the best confluence of events I could imagine.

What could go wrong?

I arrived a few days early to hang out with Jorge, and also so I could have that magical moment of connection, like you see in movies, the first time we met when I picked her up at the airport. It would be the story we'd tell our kids and all our friends about for decades to come.

Here's how it went down in my head: I'm patiently waiting in the baggage claim area when I see Mary walking through a horde of people and dragging her carry-on behind her. We stand face to face a few feet apart for just a moment and then move in for a hug that is followed by a deep and passionate kiss. The kiss is something right out of an MTV Movie Award nomination for best kiss. I shit you not. An orchestra starts playing from a distance.

"Why is there an orchestra in an airport?" she asks.

It is love, as intense as it is immediate. After the greatest weekend of my life and a few months of trying the long-distance thing, visiting each other once in Toronto once in San Francisco, we make a move to New York City. We get married a few years later and have a boy and a girl and two pups named Rocky and Bullwinkle. After I land the lead role in the new Christopher Nolan movie (which I also cowrote with the genius behind the revived *Batman* franchise) and receive a nice fat paycheck, I get us a place on Central Park West overlooking the park from the forty-fifth floor.

The here and now of the situation was a completely different picture. I was in the baggage claim area waiting for young Mary to make her way through the exit. She came out with her carry-on rolling on the floor behind her—I got that much right. We stood a few feet apart. She was awfully shy, which was cute in a we-only-Skyped-for-a-few-weeks kind of way, though in reality, our connection had already lasted more like half a year.

To be perfectly blunt: There was absolutely no spark. It was disappointing, to say the least, for both of us.

After a few days together, a few forced conversations trying to spark up some chemistry and having to share a bed like we'd been married for over fifty years—the kind of marriage where a couple thinks, *At this point in our lives, getting a divorce is just too much trouble.*

Lying on opposite sides of the bed with our backs to each other, we came to the mutual conclusion that after six months of telling each other absolutely everything there was to tell another person, we still didn't know each other at all.

I know there's a lesson here—hang on, it's coming.

The last time I saw Mary was in Jorge's apartment with her bag packed, standing next to the doorway waiting for a cab to take her to the airport. "I have something for you," she said as she handed me a book.

"What's this?" I asked.

It was a fairly thin book, weighing close to nothing, about a hundred to 120 pages in length with a black cover front and back. "The book I told you about," she said. "It tells you everything you need to know about building a brand or a blog, all the ins and outs of social media—all that jazz."

"Awesome. Thank you," I said. I watched her leave, then I closed the door behind her and opened another chapter in my life. I threw the book in my backpack next to my carry-on for my flight home the next day.

"Next time you come back to New York, I think we should get our personal training certifications," Jorge suggested. "I think we could both do well in that business, especially you." I'd never actually thought about it before, but Jorge and I did do some nasty workouts together. *Nasty* meaning "excellent" and "hardcore."

We said our goodbyes the next day and before I left Jorge told me that if I ever needed a place to regroup and reset, I should never hesitate to come and stay with him, which was, in fact, a great piece of information to have.

So now I find myself back at JFK Airport at that moment, waiting outside my gate, completely perplexed and contemplating all the events that had unfolded over the past year and how my future romantic plans all came crashing down in a few weeks. What just happened? How could I not have seen this coming?

Where did I go wrong?

The Five Gifts of the Universe

Have you ever been so sure of something that you couldn't even contemplate any other kind of outcome in your mind? And then had your expectations entirely defeated?

Sure, you have. More than likely, you're reading this book not because somehow everything seems to go your way every single time but because your life has been a bit of a conundrum. You want to be happy and free—spontaneous—but when things don't go as expected, maybe you cringe instead of celebrating a new chance to adapt.

This is how the shit happens that feels like a sucker punch. You thought you'd planned for every kind of contingency. Everything was pointing up. The door was wide open. But then, maybe, an upcoming job promotion you didn't get that you worked hard for went to the new guy. You put in the hours. You put in the years of dedication and loyalty. You were the one given glowing reviews, year after year. You were given reassurances.

What happened? New guy's dad turned out to be your boss's best friend.

Tough luck. "Maybe next year, buddy," you hear as another door closes firmly in your face. Another opportunity is taken from you.

Now, because you can't seem to catch a break, you find yourself shaking your head while staring down into an empty shot glass from which the citrus residue of tequila emanates, lightly engaging your nose, questioning what you could have done differently.

Or, maybe your expectations, like mine, had to do with a relationship. Or, maybe you have some family issues you're trying to manage.

Here's the reality: The world isn't set up to meet our expectations. The good stuff that we want doesn't always come to us as predicted. The world is very strange and weird shit happens every day; and here's something probably nobody told you as a kid because they didn't want to intimidate you or freak you out, life is a cluster fuck of twists, turns, and surprises.

But the surprises don't always suck. Sometimes what happens is far better than imagined. And sometimes circumstances that appear awful and feel devastating at the moment are just the wrapping on a gift that the world intends to give us. We have to have faith and wait a minute for the pleasant surprise inside the box to reveal itself.

There are five gifts we get whenever a window is slammed shut in our face by life: knowledge, insight, introspection, chance, and change. And when you begin to use these gifts, you will find there are more open doors than the closed one on which you can't stop focusing.

The Gift of Knowledge

To get my mind off the riddle that was my life, and because I had some time to kill, I took the book that Mary had given me out of my bag. The cover read: *Why NOW Is the Time to CRUSH IT! Cash in on Your Passion.* Immediately, I was mesmerized by the capitalized words, thinking, *Why NOT NOW?* The author credit read: Gary Vay • ner • chuk with little dots printed between syllables. My curiosity was triggered. I started reading it at the airport and again after the flight boarded. By the time my plane landed in Toronto, I had read the entire book from cover to cover.

I was still not basking in the glory of putting the week behind me. To be perfectly honest, I was far from over it. But after reading this incredibly well-written how-to formula for success in the media age, the whole idea of blogging had piqued my curiosity. I wanted to be passionate about my work! I wanted to make money doing something I enjoyed! I wanted to write! I wanted to CRUSH my life! Vaynerchuck's description of his life path stirred me up.

An interesting point of reference: Before the whole acting thing and moving to New York thing and studying with the great William Esper thing, and whatever it was I was doing in Toronto thing ever happened, I wanted to be a journalist. I had started taking journalism classes in college and for the final assignment for one class, in particular, an assignment that would count for half our grade, we were required to create a full-on magazine: ten articles with images and a cover, a real true-to-form magazine that you could hold in your hand to flip through its pages. I loved it, and the final result was a masterpiece at the college level. When I was a kid, I always loved creating stories and jotting ideas down.

This Gary Vaynerchuck fellow got me going in the same way my journalism teachers had. I was inspired, which was what I needed to take my mind off the fact that I was still feeling pretty low about the whole meeting-the-girl-of-my-dreams scenario turning out to be a fabrication layered on top of a "missing person report" poster in my mind. (Metaphors rule!) Not to mention that there was still the job that left me in a constant state of "meh" and the lack of ambition . . .

Wait, could they be connected?

My first week back home I hired a graphic designer to create a website for me, and then I went at it, writing immense numbers of words about everything and anything, but mostly fitness because it was what I knew. It was fun. A few weeks later, I had more than a dozen blog posts linked to my website.

But I still felt something was missing. Which is why I started to think about what my vision was. From then on, if I wasn't working or getting in a workout, I was spending my time sitting in various corners of bookstores reading different books.

That's how the universe—through Mary—gave me the gift of knowledge. In the pursuit of more of the same, I then stumbled on the next gift, the gift of insight.

The Gift of Insight

A month after I got home, I had what I can only describe as the most puzzling conversation I've ever had, even to this day, a conversation that seemed like it could have been a dream. This exchange completely shifted my mindset, in a moment changing the course of my life forever. You know the kind. A conversation that nudges, "The universe is working for you."

I was between shifts at the restaurant, which was located across the street from a massive two-story bookstore where I spent most of my breaks. In the bookstore, I found my way into the mindfulness and self-healing section, an area I had been paying more attention to as a result of my emotional training at the acting studio.

As I was standing there, a man walked up to me. He was a regular-looking guy, somewhere in his mid-forties, and I'll tell you, I couldn't remember his name now even if you pointed a gun at my head. But he knew an awful lot about me. Not in the manner of specific details but in enough detail to resonate with what I was feeling at that time. For the sake of context, let's call this man Bob.

My eyes fixated on the cover of some book on mindfulness, so I didn't notice the shadow cast over me when Bob approached. Standing next to me, he looked at the book I was holding and proceeded to initiate a conversation. "That's a great book."

My mind was partly elsewhere. It took me a second to realize the man next to me was talking to me. To be polite, I replied, "I'm sure it is." I flipped the book open and casually read a few pages.

Bob looked thoroughly through the section. "Mindfulness is important," he then said. "But you won't find what you're looking for here."

Now I chuckled, thinking, *What is this guy going to try to sell me?* "Oh, no?" I said. "And I suppose you have a recommendation?"

"I do," he said as he turned and oriented his attention fully toward me. "Do you mind if I tell you something?" he asked. I didn't say a word, just patiently waited to hear his sales speech. "Forget about the girl." Now he had my full attention.

"Excuse me?"

He smiled, "I see something going on inside you. Something incredible. But it's clouded by something not so incredible. There's a lot of darkness inside you right now."

At this point, I was too stunned to speak and way too intrigued to walk away, so I just stood there and listened.

He continued, "You'll go through many more dark moments in your life before you fully embrace the extraordinary." He took the book from my hand and put it back in its place on the shelf. "You're not looking for a book, but I do see that this area is where you belong. Before you can realize that, however, you'll have to find your way out of the darkness. Your answer is not here, in this city. Or in your job. And it's certainly not in this girl who is on your mind—a relationship which, by the way, is really about something else completely."

I couldn't quite tell at that moment if the guy was being sincere or messing with my head. "So, you read minds, is that it?" I asked.

"I read people," he said.

"So, what are you telling me?"

"I'm telling you that you have a very long journey ahead of you. Give yourself a chance and stop focusing on what you can't control. You'll save yourself years. Just remember what I have told you." With that, Bob walked away.

Watching him go, I had a sudden insight: *Bob was right. I've been so busy thinking about what didn't happen, that I had been missing out on the opportunities that could be happening.*

I instantly put Mary behind me, even before Bob turned away. The burden lifting off my shoulders was so heavy that immediately I felt weightless as if I could fly. *What just happened? And this sensation I'm feeling all of a sudden, what is it?* I couldn't explain it, but there was a palpable shift inside me. I felt it right there and then in that bookstore.

The gift of insight is truly powerful.

The conversation lasted no more than a minute, but its impact was huge. I honestly don't remember many details of things surrounding the conversation of that day—not a thing about what I was wearing or the book in my hand, or whether Bob was taller or shorter than me. If today, he walked right by me on the street or even knocked me over, I would never know it was the same man. But I do remember every single word he spoke to me that day. And I thought about them not just for the rest of that day, but for weeks, months, years after.

See how the universe spontaneously gave me the gift of introspection?

The Gift of Introspection

I knew I wasn't happy and that I needed to make a change—not soon, not later, but then, at that moment, standing in that bookstore. I didn't have a plan, but I certainly wasn't going to figure it out if I stayed where I was. I quit my job the same week I met Bob and gave notice to my landlord. Then I called Jorge and took him up on his offer to stay with him.

Because I had money put away, I had the means to live while I figured out my next move. This gave me some time to reflect on how I felt about everything that had occurred in the last year, from my conclusion with Mary, and in hindsight, what significance did it have with me, moving forward. With the stranger in the bookstore's words still echoing in my consciousness, "I'm telling you that you have a very long journey ahead of you. Give yourself a chance and stop focusing on what you can't control," after just a little over a year in Toronto, I booked a flight back to New York. I crammed everything I'd ever owned into a giant suitcase and traded my comfortable bed for a fold-out couch. For the time being, I called it home.

The process of introspection gives way to living spontaneously. By examining your thoughts and feelings, you begin freeing yourself from mental constraints and become more available to your true passions and new experiences.

The gift of introspection allowed me to rest my focus on doing what I loved, and it also allowed me to discover a purpose in doing it.

A few weeks later, Jorge and I committed to getting personal training certification. It made perfect sense, considering we both lived in the gym and were devoted to living our best and healthiest lives. For me, that meant eating well and building healthy habits so that I could create stronger muscles and a clearer mind. A strong work ethic was always the backbone of my efforts—that and learning new ways to improve on old tricks—so why not make a living doing everything I was already doing to change people's lives? We decided to enroll in the National Academy of Sports Medicine program as it was recognized worldwide as one of the top-level courses for fitness trainers.

I was determined to pass the certification examination on the first go and spent almost every waking hour studying when I wasn't training in the gym or blogging. Most nights, I went to the twenty-four-hour Starbucks at Columbus Circle in the early morning, around five, and studied, or I stayed there late, until two or three. I created cue cards and took them everywhere I went. I tested myself every day using the Academy's online exams until I was hitting nearly 100 percent on every try.

The day arrived that had a big circle on my calendar to highlight my exam, an appointment booked months prior. I didn't doubt in my mind that I wasn't going to ace it easily. After taking the time to examine what my mind had been focusing on, my focus was where it needed to be. I was as prepared for this as for anything I'd ever done. I was the first person there, and the first person in the room to stand up having finished the exam. I wasn't overly confident. I just knew all the answers. I waited in the next room while the proctor tabulated my results and verified that I'd passed!

I was thrilled to get my personal training career started.

The Gift of Chance

Shortly after finishing at the Academy, a serendipitous encounter as beautiful as any I have ever seen occurred that set off a chain reaction in my life. It might have been my first encounter of its kind, but it wouldn't be my last. Serendipity happens when you allow yourself to receive the gifts from the universe. When those gifts develop, a chain of events that present themselves as happy coincidences occurs.

One evening, I happened to be attending a fashion show in the Hamptons on Long Island and found myself striking up a conversation with a stunning six-foot-tall fashion model. She had recently started searching for alternative ways to lead a healthier lifestyle. Somewhere in between a few runway shows and a second or third glass of champagne, I told her about my interest in journalism and my work on my blog and explained how I had been experimenting with alternative diets.

It so happened that this model had a friend, a photographer in the fashion industry, who was starting a publication—one that would focus on diversity and aim to make an impactful message beyond fashion. He had already built a wealth of contacts and was still looking to add a few more strong writers to the magazine staff. She thought writing for her friend might interest me. A suggestion to which I said, "Hell yeah, I would be interested."

It sounded like the opportunity I'd been looking for, maybe even a little too good to be true. But then, as I thought about the serendipitous events that had been occurring since my trip to New York, I decided I wouldn't question gifts from the universe anymore. Every encounter seemed like a blessing.

Daniel, the publisher of the new magazine, sent me an email a few days later stating he had taken a look at my blog and loved my writing style. He was thorough in his email concerning his vision for the publication, describing who his intended audience was and the quality of the content he wanted, before asking me if I'd be interested in interviewing for a writing position. And I was. At the time, Daniel was vacationing in Paris, so we weren't able to meet just yet, but we tentatively agreed on my acceptance of the position and made a plan to talk in the next little while. I knew right away that this would become an incredible opportunity.

If you accept a gift of chance, it always leads to something new in your life—changes. Part of a spontaneous life is saying yes to unexpected opportunities, trusting that the changes they deliver will be positive ones that benefit you by helping you to express your potential.

The Gift of Change

Soon I would be headed back to Canada. I was tired of living out of a suitcase, never really feeling settled and at home. I wanted to plant some roots for myself.

Now I had a great new opportunity to build on a career I loved. As a writer, I would need time and patience to build my resume. If I were going to make a name for myself in journalism, I would have to find a "pond" big enough to make great connections and build a solid social network, but small enough that I wouldn't get lost in the shadow of the bigger "fish."

In addition to blogging and prospectively penning magazine articles, I was now a certified personal trainer, albeit one with absolutely no professional experience, looking to enter a growing market in the fitness industry, with lots of opportunities to grow with it. I figured if I were passionate enough about it, I could do very well as a personal trainer while building my portfolio as a journalist.

It seemed pretty obvious that the answer to my question of where I should live was always going to be Vancouver.

If I decided to continue acting, tons of features and episodic TV series were filming there at any given time, among them the *Twilight* sequels and *50 Shades of Grey*, and Netflix had several series shooting.

Vancouver also has breathtaking scenery. Beaches and mountains surrounded it. This was something my new publication would want to consider if I was to organize stunning outdoor photoshoots for their articles.

Leaving New York was never going to be easy. But I'd learned that change is inevitable. You just need to adopt the right mindset and attitude to adapt.

Hello, Vancouver.

I set three goals that needed to be addressed in order: Find a place to live, find a job, and start building my social network for the businesses of journalism and fitness. The first was easy enough to accomplish. I got a place within days in a high-rise overlooking a beach, with the natural light of dawn to wake me up and magnificent sunsets to inspire my creative flow. I was on pins and needles awaiting my first few writing assignments from Daniel.

Second goal, a job. After only a few weeks, I was hired by the city's biggest franchise gym, Steve Nash Fitness World, named after one of the best point guards and pure passers in the modern-day National Basketball Association, two-time season MVP Steve Nash, now retired. After Covid, they sold and rebranded and are now just called Fitness World. The gym had more than twenty locations spread across the city and the entire province of British Columbia. Interestingly, the particular facility that hired me, located in the downtown financial district, would soon contribute to catapulting my writing career.

Goal three, networking. After a few months of making cold calls, talking to people I met at the gym, and putting in hours and hours of service time to build my clientele, I started to make a pretty good living as a personal trainer, although nothing quite like the income I wanted just yet. Outside the gym, I was focusing on my passion for writing. This would also broaden my network of connections and give me an audience.

Daniel had returned from France. In the subsequent weeks, we exchanged several emails. The first editorial calendar of the year was released to all his staff writers. He announced that he had decided to name the magazine *Livid*—short for *Living Identity*.

This publication subsequently built itself a cult following over time, with every issue increasing the quality of the content, interviews, and images. I was there from the beginning. I wrote my first article for the premier issue in a week flat: a one-page article about my healthy lifestyle.

I remember seeing that maiden issue for the first time and flipping it open to my article. I was proud of myself. In the following issues, I would get a chance to interview some intriguing people: Meghan Currie, a yoga teacher from Vancouver with a massive following on YouTube; her channel had around 66,000 subscribers and views ranging from 100,000 to over a million per video. And trending in the world of health, New York native Vanessa Barg, known as Chocolate Girl, the founder of Gnosis Chocolate, a raw and vegan artisanal chocolate company that was one of the first of its kind. Her chocolate bars are still the best tasting I've tried.

In its second year of production, the magazine began coming out with an issue quarterly. Daniel would tell me he was constantly working with flaky writers who were always late meeting his deadlines. He had always been gracious to me with his words, commending me for getting my work in on time and the quality of my work. That year, he offered me full control of the Culture section, which at the time meant providing two six-to-eight-page editorials for each issue and finding writers to work under my supervision.

I was already setting my sights on how to improve my role. I was licking my chops at the opportunity, acceptance of which meant I now had to build my professional network to include industry talent: photographers, stylists, models, actors, producers, agencies, and makeup artists. To do these things, I was going to have to do what I'd never done before in such an industry—put myself out there.

That's when I met Liz Rosa, the best photographer I had ever come across in either Vancouver or New York. I actually couldn't believe she wasn't working in New York. She was that good. I reached out to her with an idea and to talk shop. The next issue on the editorial calendar was the Beauty Issue, and this was going to be the first editorial spread of my career. Once Liz agreed to work with me, everything else was easy, and I enjoyed watching the magic unfold.

We got models and makeup artists to work with us in exchange for the opportunity to get professional tear sheets for their portfolios. I had leverage with the agencies that managed them because I was working for a publication, so I only had to pay for studio time. This was the first editorial I'd put together that I felt I was wholeheartedly a part of from beginning to end.

I loved the process, from interviewing the models and writing the articles, to watching Liz work in the studio. It got my creative flow going. Wanting more, I started focusing on my next personal goal: how I could up my game. Out of that desire, additional changes were inevitable. New gifts rained down on me like water from the universe, filling my cup to the brim.

Liz and I eventually would collaborate on about dozen projects more, including articles on a wide array of topics ranging from censorship in the media to the evolution of technology.

Truly, my life looked almost nothing like the life I led in Toronto, and I felt much more fulfilled.

Where Do the Five Gifts Come From?

Do you play chess? It's not an easy game. If you only know the basic rules, you don't know the game at all yet, as it is highly nuanced. Everything in chess is strategy and anticipation. It is a game played by the greatest minds in the world, including mathematicians and scientists.

Navigating your life is like making moves on a chess board. You place your "pieces" in their starting positions when you go to school, get a degree, and form a career strategy, hoping everything will work out as planned. But then you find out you were taught how to play checkers, not chess. In the real world, where you are making decisions every day that affect your well-being, success, and happiness, the pieces never move quite as smoothly as you would like. The universe, which is the smartest player there is, plays by its own rules and dominates the board. Fortunately, it is more of a friend than an opponent.

Everything that happens after you make a move is a gift from the universe. Whether you decide to move your chess piece forward, backward, or sideways, you have to have faith that what happens next is for your good. If you stay alert for the signs of it, an unexpected opportunity appears. Every move produces another opportunity, and every new opportunity further enhances your awareness of the gifts the world is giving you: knowledge, insight, introspection, chance, and change.

The gifts, which are tools that can help you engineer your life, are embedded within the challenges at hand. You can perceive them with your intuition. They come from walking into your vulnerability and exposing your true self. That's how to discover your inborn strengths and talents.

When you begin to understand how the gifts of knowledge, insight, introspection, chance, and change work for you and with you, what happens is that you're not only creating new incredible opportunities, but you're also building faith in yourself. And you literally can begin to create this faith as you don't get the thing you want. In time, you will see how not getting what you wanted was the best thing that ever happened to you. You see the other side of the coin of disappointment.

By having enough faith going forward to partner with the universe and readily making additional moves when it invites you to, you will find yourself operating from a new level of power. Because the universe doesn't make sense at all, you really cannot expect this game to seem logical. Until you have evidence of your own, try to accept that what I'm telling you is true.

Make enough moves on faith, and you will begin to form a vision of what you want.

EIGHT

MY GOALS MADE ME DO IT

What's your mission in life?

What excites you when you get up in the morning? Is it that first cup of coffee you crave before you even think about checking your emails? What if you forgot you were out of coffee filters and suddenly realized you were going to have to go through your entire morning regimen without the smell of a fresh pot brewing in your kitchen, would you feel the same enthusiasm about starting your day?

Or maybe nothing excites you at the beginning of the day. Maybe you're already thinking, right as you rise from your bed, about the end of the day and that first glass of wine you have when you take your shoes off for the last time.

Does your mind immediately fill up with 10,000 thoughts per second about things that stress and bother you the moment you wake? Maybe those first conscious thoughts are about yourself. About the things you wish you had. About the person you wish you were. Or perhaps you're usually trying to hang on to a dream that feels better than your real life.

Or maybe, just maybe, you're too busy to get up—too busy scrolling through your Instagram analytics wishing for another "like" or "follow," or looking at your friends' profiles while wishing for another life. All this before you've even sat up or brushed your teeth.

OK, so that's the first five minutes of the day. And then what happens?

Bottom line, the question is this: Do you love your life and feel like you're in motion—in flow with the energy of the universe—or do you feel stuck and unhappy?

Loving your life could easily come down to feeling joyful anticipation when you get up in the morning.

Even if you don't know what excites you, I bet you have an idea of what a good day looks like. Try answering a slightly different question: Are you winning the morning on most mornings? By *winning* I mean, feeling good because you are telling yourself good things about who you are and your ability to have what you want.

I contend that what you tell yourself in the first moment of any given day can connect you to the dreams and aspirations you have for your life, no matter how small or how big they are. If you say the right things to yourself, you stand a better chance of being successful. So, are you setting yourself up to win the morning?

Outside of our relationships with the people we love, having a purpose which excites us is the thing that makes us most happy. For me, at different points in my life that thing was my acting, that was my bodybuilding, that was my writing.

What purpose excites you enough to get you out of bed?

To be human is to be a dreamer. We all want and deserve the good life that we can imagine. For some of us, having a good life means starting a family or a business; for others, it means building a better body or traveling the world and living every day like it's precious—but it also could be a combination of one or more of any of these things and others. However, when we're done dreaming, and ready to live the dream for real, every dream starts with what we do in that first moment of the day before the mind takes over.

Your mind either can work for or against you. The first moment in the morning as you're waking can be defining. In my opinion, what separates the 2 percent of people (my guesstimate) who not only feel eager to jump out of bed to make things happen but *also* have the discipline to follow through on their desires from everybody else is that they have mastered the art of visualization. This 2 percent have mastered that skill.

Most of the world walks around completely clueless of this incredible power that our minds hold, which is waiting for us to decide to harness it. From the first moment the sun shines through the bedroom window to every moment that follows, this power is at your disposal whenever you want to call upon it.

I promise that you can create a better life by understanding and beginning to master visualization. By sharpening this natural skill, you begin to create a pathway in your mind that will lead you into alignment with everything that sets your heart afire.

I promise I'm not setting you up for fairy tales and magical portals that will lead you to a life of wealth and wisdom. Sadly, magical portals are not real. I am talking about proven science. Visualization, one of the incredible abilities we each possess, occurs in the occipital lobe located at the back of the head. This region of the brain is stimulated by the imagination.[1] Whether or not you know it, you've been using visualization to get what you want your entire life.

Turning the Invisible into the Visible

After working at Fitness World for just over a year, I had a nice base of regular clients. I would train three or four people a day, making enough money to cover my living expenses, but I was only getting by. Vancouver wasn't just the most beautiful city in Canada with a high-quality of life; it was far and away the most expensive. Coming from a guy who has lived in both New York City and Vancouver, I will tell you that just getting by cannot last forever. I've seen so many people who have moved to the city with big dreams have no choice other than to eventually move back home because the pace of the work they needed to do to survive got too tiring.

Things were good in a general sense. I couldn't complain. But I loved to sleep and was a chronic morning-snooze-button guy. What excited me about the day was prolonging my pillow time a little longer.

One evening, my buddy Jeremy came up with a fun idea for three single guys on a Saturday night. My roommate and I met him at a wine and cheese bar adhering only to the instruction to bring a pad of paper and a pen with us. The three of us were all into goal setting. But we knew little about Jeremy's cryptic agenda for our evening until our glasses were full. Then he finally revealed the details.

A little about Jeremy: One of my most successful friends, he was a highly driven financial advisor in his mid-twenties who had already made partner in his firm and published a book. I liked hanging around with him because he kept me sharp. I'd had four articles published by *Livid* magazine and received a promotion to supervising other writers in my subject area, but I had been working on upping the scale of my writing dreams. We had been meeting a few times a week for black rice sushi, occasions when we would review our *wins* for the week, which was something Jeremy had started bringing into the conversation.

Wins, by definition, were the highlights of our lives, times when things we were trying to accomplish got done, or good things happened out of the blue, such as landing a new ten-session contract with a fitness client.

Three glasses of red wine were poured. Once I heard what the plan was for the evening—to make a list of our goals—I wasn't surprised at all, except for the number attached to it. "Get out your pads of paper, boys, we're each going to write a bucket list made up of one hundred items," Jeremy said. We were sitting at a long table that would give us plenty of room to write.

Thirty items seemed more reasonable. Maybe we could stretch it to fifty. But we're talking about a hundred. *How would that even work?* I thought.

There were no rules concerning what could go on the list. We could be as outrageous as we wanted to be, as long as we got to one hundred. I believe the goal of flying was even brought up—no, not flying a plane, actually flying like a damn bird. We had to think of big goals, small goals, life goals, and immediate goals, and if someone's goal was to fly like a damn bird, then great, all power to him. We also could share ideas and put the same goals as someone else on our own lists.

This is how it worked in practical terms. We broke down the creation of our lists into ten rounds of writing ten goals at a time. A three-minute timer was set, creating the necessity to capture ten ideas quickly. After that, the timer was set again, and we went around the table for an additional three minutes and said what we wrote. The point of having a time restriction of three minutes for sharing our goals was to eliminate any fabrication of items based on fear of judgment. This would encourage us to reveal what we genuinely wanted both to ourselves and the others. Five to ten minutes were factored in for table service between rounds, as we knew we would want to order at least another bottle of wine before we were done.

Remember, your brain is always working. You are always visualizing. Whether you know it or not. Whether you like it or not. When Jeremy told us his plan, I was eager to get started.

Some of my inspiration concerning the direction I was going to go with my list came from a very unusual place. A few evenings before, I'd watched a movie that probably won't be etched in stone as a classic anytime soon, but it got me thinking about a few things. The movie was *Limitless*, starring Bradley Cooper. If you haven't seen it, here's the quick rundown.

Cooper plays an out-of-work, "starving" writer, you know, a guy just getting by. He has an actual signed book contract yet has not put a single word on paper. In a nutshell, he's got a bad case of writer's block. He can't focus, has zero confidence, talks more about the book than he does actually writing it, drinks his face off, hasn't had a decent shower in a month, has just been dumped by his girlfriend, and lives in a shit hole—that's all apparent to the audience before the end of the opening credits.

I imagined his character having the imprint of his snooze button on his thumbs from hitting it so much.

The inciting incident of the plot is that this loser has a run-in with a guy he knows whom he hasn't seen in years who gives him a magic pill that awakens 100 percent of his brain's potential. Fishing for his apartment keys, he takes the pill out of his pocket, and thinks: *Why not, life can't get any worse?* He swallows the pill right as he's about to run into his landlady, who's a menacing woman.

And then events proceed as follows. After his landlady makes a stink about the fact that he's late for his rent again, *the pill hits* and a domino effect ensues. His confidence explodes, he sweet-talks the lady, and then he helps her write a legal thesis for a class she's taking that's a surefire A before he lures her into bed. Afterward, he walks into his filthy apartment, cleans it from top to bottom, then—entirely immersed in a ridiculously creative flow—begins jotting word after word onto paper.

Yadda yadda. Plot twist. Plot twist. The deal is that Bradley Cooper HAS TO take one pill a day or he'll revert to his original state. After getting his hands on another stash of these magical pills, he writes his entire manuscript in only four days (by the end of the movie, it has become a massive best-seller). He also makes hundreds of thousands of dollars on the stock market.

While our hero still has a stash of pills, his newfound intelligence and confidence enable him to go to all sorts of high-end parties and bed babes because he becomes the life of every conversation in different languages that he learns in a few days on audio while jogging in Central Park. Everywhere he goes, he meets new and exciting people and has adventures.

Pay attention. I'm just getting to the details that are relevant to my story.

In my favorite scene in *Limitless*, Cooper finds himself poised on top of a beautiful cliff overlooking the ocean in the South of France. The drop is pretty deep. All his new admiring friends are standing around him. He asks if anyone has ever jumped. They call him crazy, an accusation to which he merely returns a smile; then he squats slightly down, getting himself positioned correctly, and launches himself right off the cliff into the ocean.

When he pops his head out of the water, surrounded by such incredible beauty on the other side of the world from his home, he has a moment of clarity of what he needs to do.

The jump looked terrifying. However, it felt like it was daring and fearlessly executed.

The water looked calming and peaceful.

I was impressed and intrigued.

The movie then unfolds into a crazy plot twist that includes a billion-dollar corporate merger, a homicide in which the hero is the prime suspect, and he is being chased by a suicidal loan shark while keeping his secret from his girlfriend. And Robert De Niro is in the movie and gives an incredible performance as usual. It's a good guilty pleasure kind of flick, with many layers, but the inspiration for my list stops right at the end of the cliff jump—thirty minutes in.

First, let me tell you, I am terrified of heights. Every time I get close to the edge of a building, a mountaintop, or any other high drop, my heart rate accelerates and I can feel my body go right into fight-or-flight mode. I assume I'm going to be killed.

I couldn't tell you what it was in seeing that moment in *Limitless*, maybe it is the smile on Cooper's face or his aplomb in the slight bend of his knees and perfect pitch off the edge of the cliff, but I wanted to experience that jump on the other side of the world. I wanted to feel terrified and fearless at the same time. I wanted to feel my body freefall into that exciting, spontaneous moment and have clarity from the joy of conquering my fears.

I also loved that scene because in it I saw this guy who started off as someone who seemed never to be able to get out of his own way, taking his fate in his own hands. He was someone who not only would not jump but would never before have even found himself looking over a beautiful cliff on the other side of the world.

Many, many layers of significance made the scene resonate for me.

Let's pretend for even a moment that the movie doesn't center around taking a super pill that unlocks incredible brain activity; that in fact, what you are seeing is a guy who has unlocked all this incredible brain activity simply because he decided he was tired of just getting by, so he got his shit together, and started spotting opportunities and evidence of the life he wanted in the world around him. Could that happen in real life? And if so, how would it happen?

To me, that character becomes a master at visualization. That dive off the cliff is the apotheosis of his transformation: staring into the terrifying unknown and letting go into completely daring, fearless territory.

Back to the bucket list night. There was my inspiration for making a list of what I wanted to accomplish before I kicked the bucket certainly, but more so, for having goals and deciding what I wanted to bring into my life in the short term.

I could go on now about everything I wrote on that list; however, the very first thing I wrote on my bucket list will always stay with me.

1. *Jump off a cliff or waterfall in Costa Rica.*

I wanted my list to be detailed, to say what and where, as I knew the ideas would feel more real to me that way. On that bucket-list night, I felt like I was on fire. And the night was just beginning for me. After sharing my goals with my buddies, I took my list home and read it over again—a few times. The first time, I read it all the way through. I looked at every single goal that had come out of my head. Some items on this list included goals I'd had for many years. Some were newer goals. A few inspiring ones I took from my buddies' lists. They included, in no particular order: write a book, learn to surf, try stand-up comedy, become a top personal trainer at my gym, master muscle-ups and 90-degree push-ups, read ten books in one month, get the cover of *Men's Health* magazine (that was my dream modeling gig when I first moved to New York), see the Super Bowl in person, meet my heroes (especially Tony Robbins, Robin Sharma, and Gary Vaynerchuk), travel abroad for a few months, visit the Great Pyramid in Egypt, Machu Picchu, Bali, and Rome, spend time in the Louvre Museum, meet "my person," and a few other things too ridiculous to mention.

The second time through, I read the first twenty items.

The third time I only looked through the first five.

Then I was stuck on number 1 only.

What was it about that moment I craved so much? Was it the fearlessness of the jump? Was it the idea of being so far away from the world I knew?

Maybe it was something more. Maybe it was the idea of everything I valued and wanted to bring into my life coalescing in a single moment of complete unknown and freedom. That was the freedom I craved.

Often the simple process of clarifying why we want to achieve a particular goal is enough to light a fire under our asses, so we don't keep putting it off. My whys in this case were as follows.

First, because cliff jumping (or jumping from the top of an epic waterfall) was not simply outside my comfort zone, it was *way* outside it. I wanted to feel the fear and say fuck it and walk into it regardless—not to look death in the face, but to smile at life and embrace the moment. When you feel the excitement of the moment, it's as if nothing exists besides that moment, because you are so present. It's spontaneous.

And second, why Costa Rica? Well, I could tell you it was just a random destination, but it wasn't. I had always wanted to travel to Costa Rica. Its beauty in photos was breathtaking. The words *pura vida* ("pure life") are synonymous with Costa Rica. Jumping felt like the freedom I wanted. Not only did I want to feel the rush of spontaneity after leaping high up into the beautiful sky and falling into nature's greatest gift, the ocean, but I also longed to be present while exploring a completely new and beautiful surrounding.

The next morning, I woke up, and the strangest thing happened. My alarm went off, but I didn't hit the snooze button. My eyes remained shut. But I didn't crave the usual extra hour of sleep. I didn't crave the first sip of my coffee. I didn't think about my schedule for the day. I didn't think about anything stressful. I just stayed there in my bed for a minute longer than usual, and suddenly there I was, standing on that cliff in Costa Rica. I felt the wind hit my face. I heard birds flying above. I felt absolute fear running all over my body as I looked down to the water, possibly as far as sixty feet below.

Mind you, this was the first moment of the day. I didn't want to sleep. I'm not sure how seriously I took the idea of it happening, but I wanted to stay immersed in the visualization of that moment a little bit longer. I knew that I wasn't in any position to create that experience. At least not then. Jumping off a waterfall in Costa Rica was undoubtedly my top goal, but before I could take such a trip, I needed to set myself up in a better financial position.

What I love in looking back at the entire bucket-list process is that I now saw a path in which I could put myself in that position. I saw the path of the person I wanted to become who was able to put himself in that position. Seeing myself as an elite personal trainer for my career of choice meant I would be self-realized, and I saw that I would experience the growth that comes with hard work and dedication. Being a top personal trainer in my company would play its role in jumping off a waterfall in Costa Rica.

Over the next few months, I had an unforeseen motivation to work extra hard at the gym: I'd decided that I couldn't just say I wanted to be the top trainer and wish upon a pretty star. I had to put in time and effort. In making this decision, I created measurable goals for myself and a set of standard behaviors to which I would adhere.

I thought long and hard about what that would look like. *What does it mean to be a top personal trainer?* I reflected on this question every morning when I woke up. Though I would have loved to sleep a little longer, I would stay in bed and daydream about who I had to be *that day* to achieve my goals. The images I saw in my mind's eye felt just as real as my visualization of standing at the top of a waterfall in Costa Rica.

Mentally, I broke down several goals that originated on my bucket list into smaller objectives, and then I took action. For example, to bolster my professional credentials, I attended several certification courses, including Kettlebell Level 1, TRX Suspension Training, Myofascial Release Techniques, Olympic Lifting, and Squat Assignments.

To add a little perspective to the fitness business: Most new trainers have an expectation coming out of the gate that everything will be given to them. They imagine having a full schedule of clients on day one. Not even close. Finding clients is a hustle. It's going to talk to people, building relationships, communication skills, and experience. Anybody can be a trainer. But very few find success doing it.

I spent more time talking to people and offering them complementary sessions. I focused on listening more closely to what they were telling me instead of waiting for my turn to speak, which helped me to cultivate more empathy and understanding of their needs. I learned that most times when they told me no, their rejection of what I was offering came either from fear or from lack of recognizing the value of the service I would deliver. So, I was practicing being empathetic and being clearer in explaining the value of working with me.

As I spent more time talking with people, my closing rates increased. Within only a few months of setting my overarching work goal, my personal habits were transformed. I was the first person at the gym at 6 AM and one of the last ones there at night. I put in more hours, booked more appointments, and decided to ditch any excuse about being too tired, frustrated, or overwhelmed.

There was an annual gym ceremony where an honor known as the President's Award was given to employees who had met high standards for their role as a salesperson, group trainer, manager, district manager, or personal trainer. As a personal trainer, to receive this exclusive honor meant you were bringing in a minimum of $100,000 per year, an accomplishment achieved by less than 7 percent of the personal trainers in the entire company.

On the first day of a new month, the regular team meeting at the gym proved to be an auspicious occasion for two reasons. First, the district manager who hired me was sitting in. Second, it was announced that the top trainer in the entire company that month would be awarded an $800 mountain bike, which was a prize I very much wanted.

I wanted to challenge myself to win the bike, so I decided I would put myself out there. After the meeting, I approached the district manager and my branch manager and proclaimed I would win that bike. I had never finished as a top trainer in the company before, or even in the top ten. Due to my persistence, I finished out the month with twenty-two training contracts closed—fourteen with new clients and eight with returning clients. It was the equivalent of $18,000 in sales, a club record. That won me the brand-new mountain bike, and it became the second month in what would subsequently become a stretch of seventy months in a row that I never fell below 100 percent of my monthly sales target. With this accomplishment, I inaugurated five straight years on the company's President's List.

The most important thing was that I started not only accomplishing various tasks and goals, but I also started to become the person I was visualizing myself being at the end of the journey. The biggest part of being that person was never in the numbers, the honors, and the records; it was in the influence a trainer has on the people the trainer works with every single day, helping them to improve every aspect of their lives. I measured this influence by the smiles I saw on the faces of the people I trained.

For a while, I forgot about the first goal on my bucket list. But it was still there, latently resting deep in my sub-conscious mind. You can be sure of that.

As you know, I was incredibly inspired when I saw Bradley Cooper cliff dive in *Limitless*. But the attraction of that scene for me—as I came to realize—stemmed from a compelling desire to overcome a fear of heights so intense that I didn't even dare look over the edge of a building if I was on the roof. (I still have this fear.) During my analysis of this goal, I could see that understanding its appeal was more important to its accomplishment than understanding the intermediate steps to accomplish it, like buying a plane ticket and making a hotel reservation, finding a guide to take me to the cliffs, and so on.

We have to make some goals happen through effort, but there are occasions when we accomplish the goal effortlessly. An opportunity to go to Costa Rica arrived exactly one week after my first record-breaking month, just after I had received a generous commission that made it seem plausible to go on a little adventure for the soul.

While scrolling down through my Facebook newsfeed, quite quickly, with all the millions of data my mind was running through, my eyes caught a glimpse of something that they might not have caught a year before. I scrolled back up, and I saw that Meghan Curry, my favorite yogi, had posted a notice about an upcoming two-week yoga retreat in Costa Rica.

I immediately had the feeling again that I was standing at the top of that cliff. I closed my eyes and felt every sensation of being on that cliff in my body and mind. I felt the fear wash away. I wanted that experience! Without hesitation, I contacted the woman running the retreat and made arrangements to meet her the next day to give her a deposit to secure my place on the trip. A few months later, I was on a plane to the tropical rainforest in Central America.

I didn't know anybody on day one. The group consisted of twenty of us, mostly in our twenties, five guys and fifteen girls. Most of the girls came from a yoga training course that had just ended. As you can probably imagine, I wasn't complaining. Everybody was nice and ready for adventure.

The first week, we practiced yoga twice a day; and if we weren't in a yoga class, it was a safe bet we were surfing. This was my first time on a surfboard—another item I could cross off my bucket list. The food was great. The weather was impeccable. It was fantastic, but no word was spoken of a waterfall.

The second week, we went on a hike, and I learned that our trail would bring us to Montezuma Waterfalls. The Montezuma Waterfalls in Costa Rica are three separate waterfalls, one above the next. The first one was the easiest to jump, as its height is merely the length of a swimming pool, about fifteen-feet tall. All eighteen of us from the group, which was made up of four guys and fourteen girls, made the first jump into a nice deep pool of water that was perfect for swimming and relaxing.

The middle waterfall, which had roughly a forty-foot drop, was hidden on the edge of this pool. The water pressure on the edge was much more intense than it was above the top waterfall, making the prospect of jumping more frightening to me. Before we attempted this jump, our tour guide forbade us to attempt jumping down the third waterfall beyond it, as the third fall had claimed more than a dozen lives. (I did say be fearless, *not insane.)*

Everybody decided to skip the second jump and stay and enjoy the pool except a few of us. As I stood on the rock looking beyond the edge to the water at the bottom, contemplating the jump, all my fears showed up. I was terrified. I looked back at everybody else having the time of their lives splashing in the pool, carefree and risk-free.

"Are you going to do it?" I asked one guy who was looking right at me.

"You're crazy if you think I'm going down there," he replied. I laughed and had a very real moment right then and there. I was actually about to cross off item one on my bucket list. I felt an overall release of freedom. And I thought, *Now I have to jump.* I smiled at him, looked forward, bent my knees slightly to get myself into position to jump, and then I leaped from that waterfall in Costa Rica.

Goal Achieved: Jump Off a Waterfall in Costa Rica

Let's talk science. Your beautiful brain has a system of neurons that are constantly working to filter information thrown at you. This system is called the (pronounce it slowly, and you'll have it) *reticular activating system.*

The first thing you need to know about the RAS, for short, is that it has no off-switch, so it is making choices about what to let through in every moment. In the context of how you think about yourself and your abilities, it constantly points out evidence that supports both your beliefs and your fears.

For example, if you think you're a loser, you're going find evidence that supports this idea, and you're going to find ways to act on it. The word *loser* will seem imprinted on the inside of your skull. You're going to prove your fears and nasty self-judgments. And if you think the world is unfair, your RAS will support that belief.

Your brain can only handle so much. If it took in every piece of data to analysis and decipher, the top of your head would either explode like a popping balloon or your brain would melt like bubbling-hot jalapeno Swiss cheese in a panini press.

OK, you can't turn it off; however, you can learn to control it. Understanding how the RAS works is vital to mastering the powerful skill of visualization, which is one that experts say only a tiny percentage of the world's population will ever master.[2] To succeed as a visualizer, you must train your brain to change the filter in your head.

The first step in reprogramming the RAS to support better beliefs about your ability to get what you want is to decide what you want. This is where the lessons we've already discussed come into play. Both short-term and long-term goals work. Get very specific with any one goal, using as much sensory detail as possible. What emotions are you drawing up? What does the picture of success look like in your head? Once you've got it, every morning right as you wake up, stay in bed with your eyes remaining closed and start to visualize that picture in your head and feel it in your body. Make the images come alive.

Make sure you do this first thing in the morning before you do anything else or think of anything else. It's important you get very specific and form a strong emotional connection to the image of success at the goal because doing it in the morning is going to be challenging if you've been hitting snooze for a long time (like I used to do). You'll be fighting off many addictions when you begin this exercise. Make yourself a promise that you will do this. This skill needs constant honing to develop it into something powerful.

By investing the first few minutes in the morning to visualizing your dreams, you begin to change the filter of your reticular activating system. It is now encoding every picture you draw and every burst of joy you feel when you truly feel the image as a memory. These new "memories" are changing the filter so that your brain will create a platform on what to do going forward.

After a while, your brain knows how to do whatever it is that you want to do. You will improve on the skills needed. You will see opportunities. You will know how to plan better. You will know all the steps you need to take because in your memory you've already gone through the process of accomplishment. Your RAS is now supporting the belief in your precise outcome. It grows in your mind. Your thoughts begin to expand. And your beliefs move outside your comfort zone. Then your actions. Life becomes spontaneous as you shift your energy forward into the beautiful unknown.

What excites you when you get up in the morning? Close your eyes and ask yourself that question tomorrow morning. Train your brain to feel what it will be like at the moment you achieve a deeply desired goal, one that makes your heart shine. Let your brain start carving out a path for you to reach this destination. Set it on a mission to achieve that goal.

Now, Write Your Bucket List

Grab a pen and paper. Don't make this process complicated. Put the numbers one through twenty on the left-hand margin of the page and then write your list. It can be a good idea to set the timer on your phone for ten minutes and then go. If you've got a buddy or two around, then you can do it simultaneously and read your lists to one another. Try not to judge. Red wine optional.

NINE

THE STRUGGLE IS YOUR LIFE

Are you resilient?

Life is a miracle. It's precious and extremely fragile. But so damned unpredictable that you know what else? Life can be a son of a bitch. It can put you on the ground, break your heart, and tear your soul in half.

And it doesn't stick around to answer questions or give you reasons—it just hits and keeps on hitting, and then it will leave you lying there and walk away, with its hands washed of you.

That's life. No matter how strong we think we are or how invincible we feel, no one is invulnerable to how hard life can hit us.

And let me tell you something else. There's nothing quite like being rushed to the hospital in the back of an ambulance with your body broken, your soul torn asunder, and nothing but darkness around you to give you just a little perspective into the madness of life.

Trust me on that.

But there's something else, an untapped genius within life's perpetual madness. Something beyond the darkness, blanketed by our suffering and when realized, aligned with the soul of human virtue.

May 27, 2017, was a significant day in my life. Because on this day, a moment in time would stand still for me. Everything in the world stopped as if I was in the middle of a scene from an X-Men movie and Professor Charles Xavier, with his ability to freeze minds, had effectively stopped everything from moving.

I was coming down a bike pathway off a heavily trafficked bridge on a beautiful Saturday morning to join friends at the beach for an entire day that would consist of doing absolutely nothing without a worry in the world. After six months of nonstop downpours of rain unlike any the city had experienced, which included a record thirty days straight of rain back in October, summer had finally come and put a smile on everybody's face. I couldn't wait to get out on the beach and generate some much-needed vitamin D from soaking in the sunshine.

And then, just as I was coming upon a lining of trees next to the bike lane—a blind spot—I heard voices from behind the trees screaming "Stop!" At that moment, the area encompassed in the blind spot became visible, and I could see, about a foot away from me, the head of a biker dropped down and speeding at about forty miles per hour downhill aiming right at me—cutting off my path. Time stopped.

Right before time froze, life was great. It was amazing. I was invincible, strong, and successful with tons of friends. In that instant, I knew I was about to get hit. This guy's bike was about to collide with mine, and I would be T-boned and sent flying through the air. I also knew that there was absolutely nothing I could do to stop it. My life was about to be not so great. It felt like a moment that stood apart from time.

Until the next moment.

And then time unfroze.

Everything went black.

Silence.

Darkness.

You know those stories we sometimes hear about freak accidents involving careless drivers sideswiping other cars or pedestrians, or of a falling beam that accidentally drops from a construction site just when someone is walking right beneath it? The difference between being in the wrong place at the wrong time and a close call is always mere seconds.

When you hear those stories, do you think, *Shit, that sucks, but it could never happen to me?* Well, it does suck. And it can happen to anybody.

Everything happened so quickly. One moment I was riding this incredible wave called life, and the next my life was changed. Disrupted. I lay on the ground for a few minutes, unconscious and surrounded by shadows, my bike broken in half, aware in a distant, absent way of the faint sound of an ambulance approaching. As I regained consciousness, I was so disoriented that I was in a complete fog. My ears kept ringing nonstop. Because of the blow to my body, the shock to my system, and the massive amount of adrenaline running through my body, I didn't feel any pain.

That would come later.

The blow to my face broke and dislocated my nose. One eye was shut due to massive swelling around the entire right side of my face. A deep cut underneath it would require over ten stitches to treat. Through the one eye that I could barely open a sharp flash of light came into my field of vision. It was the flashing light on the roof of the ambulance.

In the ambulance, I could sense that something was severely wrong with my right leg. It had grown nearly four times in size. Even trying to move it slightly was like trying to move an eighteen-wheeler off the ground. The EMTs urged me to lie still on their gurney.

As I lay in the emergency room, waiting for the doctor to come back with the results of my CT scan, I contemplated the damage. My face felt like it got knocked around a few times with a baseball bat. But being there alone actually may have been the worst part of the experience. Every gut-wrenching emotion you can imagine was painfully present: anxiety, depression, anger. All I could think was: *Where are my friends?*

They stayed on the beach.

I've never felt more alone in my life.

My mind started spiraling with all kinds of anxieties and fears. I imagined every single, worst-case scenario possible, many exaggerated: *Surgery is certain. I had a concussion/head trauma/internal bleeding/spinal trauma/a broken leg of some sort. I'll never walk again.*

Like I said, exaggerated thoughts.

I won't be able to train, so there goes my body and everything I've ever built.

My face is deformed.

Forget summer, forget 2017, forget my seventy-month sales streak—that's all but likely snapped.

Why did this happen? I was happy. Did I bring this on myself? But why me? Why is this happening to me? Everything was going so well! I had a good job, friends, and now I can't move, and I'm in an extraordinary amount of pain (which would get so much worse in the coming hours, once the adrenaline wore off), *and I'm here waiting for the doctor without a clue what the CT scan will reveal. I'm going out of my mind!*

I just lay there staring up at the wall.

Fuck my life.

"Your nose is broken," the doctor told me.

"Thanks, I knew that. What else?"

"And you broke your patella in three pieces." *The goddamned kneecap broke.* I stopped thinking then. I couldn't register anything in my brain anymore. Everything was so real. I just lay there in complete silence after that.

I would say I have a very high tolerance for pain. That night, once the adrenaline fully left my body, searing pain started to surface. I felt more pain coming from my knee than I could have ever imagined possible, and then, double that. I cursed the skies. I cursed everything I ever believed in. That night, as I lay there in the darkness, completely vulnerable,

I could barely move. I was in agonizing pain. The reality of my situation hit me.

I could feel myself free falling into a dark hole.

What the fuck am I going to do now?

The next day I met with the head of Orthopedics. She took out a notepad and drew a circle with a peace sign in the middle of it. "That's your knee," she told me. The CT scan had revealed a solid break right down the middle of my knee in the formation of a peace sign. It had broken and separated into three pieces.

There was a silver lining. "You won't need surgery," she told me.

"How is that possible?" I asked.

"The muscles surrounding your knee were strong enough that at the time of impact they automatically seized up and held the bones together," she explained. "All you have to do now is let the muscle heal on its own."

"For how long?"

"Hard to say—four, maybe five months, plus time for physiotherapy once your muscles regenerate their cells. Of course, everybody is different. You're athletic, so it's possible that you'll heal quicker."

No surgery was the best possible news I could have received for what I otherwise identified as one of the worst days of my life—and as you know, I've had my share.

The Unstoppable Force of Our Mindset

The first week after my accident, I could barely move around my apartment. Every morning I woke from a night of deep sleep into another daily battle. I could barely move and having to rely on doing everyday things, such as using the bathroom and washing up the kitchen, was the most challenging. Every time I looked out the window and saw a beautiful summer day, I got more depressed. I felt isolated.

Because of the solitude and my inability to be able to move around, every day I felt a little more broken, as if I was slowly losing my mind, bit by bit.

I was content with feeling thoroughly sorry for myself. It just seemed easier that way. I didn't want to care about anything. But in the middle of all my self-pity, something shined through the following week. I received more than twenty phone calls and close to forty text messages—everybody I knew, old friends and new, was offering to help. People took turns coming over with groceries and making me dinner. Even the actor Patrick Warburton, whom I'd trained that year, took time away from filming his Netflix series, *A Series of Unfortunate Events*, to surprise me with a visit. He brought me a bag of hard candy from Whole Foods.

My mom called me a few times a day from the other side of the country. My good friend Seth took time almost every day to come to see me or to call. He drove me to every one of my hospital appointments. At times I felt alone, but I was rarely actually alone. This experience of being supported rekindled my spirit. Even when we feel completely alone and vulnerable, connection is so powerful it can give us a new sense of purpose. Another human being has the power to give us light when we want to live in the dark.

During my period of recovery from the accident, I felt stressed about the uncertainty. I was in constant pain. I was going through waves of depression. I often thought about Alex, who had taken his life a decade earlier, and what he must have gone through when he felt depressed, thinking he was all alone before he made that fateful decision. Though he may not have known it, Alex wasn't alone, and neither was I. My friends were my shining lights, and, because of them, I decided I was not going to allow my accident to crush my spirit.

I wanted to be mad at the world, especially at the guy who recklessly hit me. I wanted to live in the darkness of my depression, but the amazing people in my life weren't feeding into my broken spirit and sadness. They brought me cheer and optimism.

When these horrifying, uncontrolled, life-changing things happen to you, and you can't understand what you did to deserve them, and you can't find anything to be grateful for, depression sets in. All your anxiety, judgments, doubts, and fear come out.

You go into a black hole. It becomes your belief that you will live in absolute darkness for the rest of your life. Your feelings of trauma may be so strong that you program your RAS to believe that the universe is doing this to you on purpose. You may lose faith. Your intuition may be switched off. Your vision can disappear in the darkness. You can feel as if you're stuck in quicksand. There may seem to be no escape.

It would take something superhuman to pull you out of such a hole. Something unimaginable to the naked eye of your inner narrative. This power could change your life. It will shift you toward something greater than whatever plunged you into darkness.

See, the truth is, regardless of how many friends you have who are there for you or how many you don't, it makes no difference in the real world because the only person in the world who can pull you out of the depths of despair is you. The only person who can develop the courage to accept reality and not let the circumstance dictate the outcome is you.

Try to imagine what it would be like if everything in your life came to you without any tests or obstruction. Imagine you didn't experience any hardships growing up. If that were the case, then you wouldn't know how pain feels. You would've never experienced failure.

If you got everything you could ever want. It was just there, every single time—that easy—life would be a fucking dream. Literally!

Because what inevitably happens? One day, unexpectedly, life comes at you harder than you have ever experienced.

Because *shit happens*. To us all. The form is different for different people. Perhaps you lose your job from a sudden pandemic that shuts down the world. That happened to me. Perhaps the stock market plummets. Your entire life savings are wiped out overnight. The economy collapses. That happened to tons of people in the last recession. The stress of a downturn could be so severe that you lose your health, then lose your hope. Or you lose your husband or wife.

If you're accustomed to a fairy-tale life, in the face of adversity you could break because you have never experienced any hardship or developed the habits of resilience. Without needing to overcome obstacles, your beliefs would be limited to how easy life is and always will be. Anything else would simply not be in your plan. You would have absolutely no clue about this remarkable power that you can tap into anytime you wanted: your conscious mind.

Because you wouldn't have the mindset.

If anyone can figure out what to do, it's going to be me. Everything always works out for me. I get stronger when my back is against the wall. That mindset.

You wouldn't have had the conditioning from your intuition, your emotional intelligence, or your faith to respond to a crisis spontaneously on the spot. Each of these human qualities is something that we can use to better our frame of mind. How could you build an emotional connection to a vision if it was not powerful enough to pull you out of the darkness when life tests you?

Life is not a constant state of feeling like you are over the moon, and everything that ever stressed you has just magically disappeared. That kind of life doesn't exist. Our reconditioning is directly related to overcoming hardships. You cannot experience growth without struggle. You cannot become strong without confronting resistance. You have no reason to change unless you're challenged.

When terrible things happen to us, we can lose momentum, lose our comfort, and lose what we know, and the hardest thing to do is to keep pushing through. But we also can turn misfortune into triumph because pain is ultimately our best friend. You may not know it when you feel as if life is slipping from your fingers, but for the very maturation of your being, your personal evolution into the strongest you that you can be, pain is your *best friend.*

Every time life knocks you on your head, the knock was sent for a reason. It contains a series of lessons on how to improve yourself, to deepen your connection to yourself, to show people your strength, or to teach you to focus on what matters. Overall, making choices based on the belief that something great will come out of this is a phenomenally resilient approach to life. An empowering belief.

The true task ahead is to reclaim your mental power.

Six Essential Beliefs for When Your Back Is Against the Wall

When you're in a struggle to overcome a crisis, your true task is managing your mindset. Go internal. You can transform any facet of your life if you begin by changing your mindset and embrace the following six beliefs.

Belief #1. Change Is Up to You

Will your situation get easier? Maybe not at first. Some days will be harder than others. Some days will feel like hell. But while it is easier to blame our circumstances for all the terrible things that happen to us, it takes courage to look at ourselves and ask the tough questions, beginning with: *What the hell am I going to do?* Answering this question and taking responsibility for solving our problems usually requires us to embrace a level of discomfort we have never previously faced. Remember, you are hardwired by millennia of survival on earth to adapt. If you want to take control of your fate, you will be required to live with a certain level of discomfort.

Belief #2. You Are Much Stronger Than You Think

Remember how we're made? Humans were created with an internal compass to guide us: our intuition. Although we may feel vulnerable, our intuition is always doing its best to lead us exactly where we want to go. This ability makes us strong. You have more control over your life than you may think.

Belief #3. Pain Is Tolerable, Suffering Is Optional

Suffering is an internal response to things that happen to us. Two people can experience the same event, and one may only feel the instant pain, but not choose to let it define him or her, whereas the other will use the pain to design a pattern of suffering that will formulate every decision he or she makes from then on.

If we are courageous, then we can learn to tolerate pain in the short term without suffering extensively or we can ask for the help we need to overcome our pain.

Suffering is self-defeating.

Belief #4. A Positive Mindset Can Be Reinforced by Good Habits

Make no mistake about it, our habits and our mindsets are connected. Positive daily habits keep the mind and body sharp and attuned with spirit. If you have the mindset that you can overcome struggles and face adversity, then you will likely be doing so by adopting helpful habits. These habits become you, and they define you as they get ingrained in your neural pathways.

Belief #5. Societal Conventions Are Irrelevant to Your Situation

Society has always put up barriers to certain types of people, but arbitrary barriers like gender, race, ethnicity, and sexual orientation don't have to limit you. The numbers may be against you. The majority creates the rules, but rules can and do change. Some people are born talented. Some people win the genetic lottery. Some people are born into wealth and influence. And others aren't. Society may tell you: You are not the "right kind of person." You're "not tall enough." You're "not good-looking enough." You're "too weak." You failed "too many times." But you don't have to listen to the rules and conventions. What your mind and body can accomplish goes beyond what any belief or fear can dictate.

Belief #6. Struggle Is an Inevitable Part of Life

Every time you're in pain, it is useful to remember that it holds a lesson that could contribute to making you a more remarkable person. I will say that again: Every pain is another lesson. You can become someone remarkable, even superhuman. If we learn from them, our trials can make us more resilient. We have the power to transform. That was the lesson my father showed me that first day I saw him in the cancer ward. By rising to the challenge of his cancer, my father rewrote his narrative and accepted that struggle was now part of his life, and he used it to transform and become stronger. I would face similar challenges as my father when I was lying in the hospital after my accident.

A spontaneous life is created in the valley of pain and struggle as much as it is on the mountaintop of joy and accomplishment. Sometimes it takes a tragedy for us to develop humility or compassion for somebody else, or to truly make us grateful for our lives and the moments we are gifted to be with our friends and loved ones—or to be capable of enthusiastically pursuing a noble purpose.

Each morning, wake up, and after you visual the life you want, say thank you and be grateful for your struggles. This is your life. Once you realize this, you can begin the process of retraining your subconscious mind to support you in making it the best life.

PART III

WHEN YOU AND THE WORLD DANCE TO THE SAME BEAT

TEN

THE POWER OF WRITING SHIT DOWN

Are you willing to go internal?

When was the last time you checked in with yourself to ascertain what was going on inside you? Have you ever looked at yourself and admitted how you're really doing?

Wait . . . I checked my Instagram. I'm good!

Let's be honest, the only thing that matters is that your TikTok and Instagram posts say you're great, right? If our posts make us look like we're fan-fucking-tastic, then we have nothing to worry about. True?

No.

Have you ever heard the saying, "I hope your life is as good as you pretend it is on Instagram"?

Welcome to the world we live in, in which it's completely okay to feel like crap and question everything as long as you keep your feelings bottled up inside you. You know, as long as you catch yourself from that perfect angle, against the light, on your good side.

And don't forget to smile. That's important. You get more likes when you smile.

But that other stuff, nobody wants to hear that. Maybe you don't have to tell the world you feel like a bum hole, but it might be to your benefit to tell yourself, *Hey, it's not alright that I feel this way all the time.*

In case you thought I was 100 percent courageous and never suffered after my explanation of strength in the last chapter, let me set you straight. I was in denial about the raging inferno of emotions about to erupt inside me.

I started to recognize I was engaging in a slow-motion downfall after coming back from my bike collision. I knew I was going down a destructive path and that the happiness and confidence I had felt about the speed and success of my recovery were slipping through my fingers. But I didn't know what to do about it, so I tried to ignore what was happening.

In retrospect, my bike accident was the best thing to ever happen to me. At the time, it seemed like my strength had been taken away from me. Even once I was back at work, I couldn't escape the sensation that something was wrong or that danger was at hand. I didn't realize it yet, but I needed to make a major change in my life.

You need a change if you:

- Can't stop thinking about the past.

- Have zero ambition. Nothing drives you anymore.
- Have developed an addiction to a substance, a behavior, or even your comfort.
- Are going through the motions of life simply for the sake of surviving.
- Spend time in an environment that has become toxic to your growth.
- Can't seem to focus on anything for too long.
- Find reasons not to make relationships work.
- Are comparing yourself constantly to other people.
- Are seeking external approval constantly.

I was exhibiting a lot of these symptoms.

Telling myself I would change my behavior the next day was becoming a habit in itself. It gave me a momentary sense of gratification each time I made this promise to myself because I believed I would. Hence, I was caught in a vicious, self-defeating loop.

Do you know when I discovered this?

I discovered this when I started writing shit down.

I have been journaling for a while, mostly on and off, and this has benefited me greatly in many areas of my life. It has been a big factor in changing my life for the better. When I first started journaling, I remember getting excited about it—waking up early and writing about all the great things I wanted to learn—I was especially hyped up about personal development. I was like, *Hell yeah, self-growth rocks! Let's write this down!*

But the moments I was writing about weren't always awesome. We all have our share of life-sucks moments between the awesome ones. What I noticed from being attentive in my behavior was when those not-so-great moments occurred, for whatever reason, I frequently wouldn't journal about them. Sometimes because I didn't feel like it and sometimes because the thought of journaling never crossed my mind. When I was feeling stressed or angry, I would be consumed by my old habits, which were designed to help me be comfortable, even if they weren't particularly wholesome.

Because I didn't journal when I was in a down mood, I never saw the opportunity in front of me to reflect and grow from my discomfort, so my negative feelings festered. During my recovery from the bike accident, I had a lot of free time on my hands. I finally took notice that this was my pattern, funnily enough by journaling about it; I committed right then and there that I would journal every day no matter how I felt, either at the beginning or the end of the day. I typically reread my journal entries weekly on Sundays.

To the present day, I have maintained this commitment.

The reason I couldn't get around my bad habits over the previous year, despite being fully recovered from my physical injuries and back to being successful as a trainer, was that I was continually feeding off my fear and anger.

By committing myself to journal every day, I discovered that I had been angry so many times in my life, first from my father's death, and then my best friend's suicide, and again from not making it as an actor, and this emotion had always fueled my competitive drive. I found that I only felt complete if I was "winning" at life. All my success as a personal trainer, as a journalist, as somebody who is always looking for that next challenge had come from that same competitive drive. This belief was the script my inner narrative had followed for most of my life. To succeed and be happy, I told myself I always had to be winning, or else I was "nothing."

Now, when the speeding biker hit me and sent me to the hospital, I found myself left in a state of complete vulnerability that I had never been in before, and I couldn't hide my anger any longer. I initiated a writing routine to soothe my upset and reflect on my life and future. Once I was back at work and recovered, I journaled every morning and every evening. I wrote down every thought I had, every vision I felt.

For example, I reflected on my memory of standing on top of that second waterfall in Costa Rica and the intimacy of that moment. That feeling of being suspended in time. No past. No future. Just now. When everything is connecting. That feeling of pure flow that runs through your mind and body during peak experiences.

I wrote down every word. Because I knew I wanted to make a change.

Then an opportunity for change spontaneously occurred.

I had an altercation with a young gym member one Saturday afternoon. Blond hair tied in a knot. A very large temperament. Roger was a bully who'd had many verbal run-ins with other members and personal trainers since I'd started working at the gym. He often used dehumanizing language with people he disagreed with—it seemed to me, as a means of indulging in self-validation of his superiority. Normally, I kept my distance, and we never talked. But he decided to change that this afternoon.

Here's how it went down.

Picture this. I have a series of exercises set up on a universal machine—the weights and seat heights adjusted for my client—and she is on the floor next to our station doing sit-ups between sets, with her towel hanging off a bar and her water bottle right next to it. Roger walks over to this station and proceeds to remove the towel and move the bar that we have set up, disregarding that we are clearly using the station.

I watch what he is doing—he doesn't look at me—and I am already feeling the stress of having to deal with him.

"We have one more set, and then you can use it," I tell him politely.

Roger responds in an aggressive tone, "Yeah? Well, go do something else." Again, without eye contact.

I walk over and kneel to change the weight. *Probably it would be best to walk away right now*, I remember thinking.

Roger now kneels, grabs my wrist, and pulls me in. Now he is looking right at me, and he says, "Hey dick wad, somebody's going to get hurt."

I am a little too stunned to react quickly. But I easily outweigh Roger by about thirty pounds. I take a moment to contemplate what might be going through this guy's head. I would be lying if I told you that the thought of knocking this guy out, with one easy shot to his face, didn't cross my mind for just a moment, but I could feel his hand trembling. He is evidently nervous, just a little boy trying to bluff his way through life. I am aware he is trying to provoke me to act.

Because I have a heightened sense of awareness that is very present, my better sense prevails. Looking at the mirror, I notice that two members are standing behind me watching everything. I let go of the pin.

I am so enraged that I decide to file a complaint.

Can you see the scene in your mind's eye? Feel the stress?

After the Roger incident, a report was sent to management, and an investigation was conducted. They interviewed anybody in the company who knew Roger, including trainers and members he'd had run-ins with before, establishing a pattern of behavior. The investigation went on for a few days, after which it was concluded that his membership should be revoked. He was gone.

I remember how happy I was when I heard the news. I journaled about how happy I was the moment I found out. It was probably the first thing that made me happy ever since before the bike accident.

But then I woke up the next morning and I didn't feel quite as happy anymore. I reread my journal entry about the outcome. And after I read it, I didn't feel anything.

Everything started to connect. I was happy because I was "winning" again—just not in the way I knew would truly bring out the best in me. I was feeding into my old belief system. What I was not able to feel had nothing to do with Roger. That realization got my attention. He had triggered something that was buried deep inside me—and if he had been able to trigger it, then there was always the possibility that I would be triggered again and again by something else.

It is easy to find yourself stuck and not realize how it has happened. To counteract this state, you have to work on yourself and diligently find and disarm the triggers, buried like landmines. And I believe in constantly working on yourself because change is constant and we need to adapt.

Reading my journal entry from the day before my encounter with Roger prompted me to do something differently—to break my patterns of thought and behavior.

My uncomfortable change started the next morning.

My alarm went off. I was still hovering inside a dream. The details of the scene were clear: *I'm on a beach, somewhere far away—away from city life, away from civilization, in complete solitude, surrounded by the calming beauty of the ocean. I can see birds flying in a line in a clear sky, passing in front of a beautiful sun that is rising over a tropical setting. I can feel a breeze on my face.*

Even fully awake, it was as if I was still there—emotionally connected to that moment—but this was not any emotion with which I was familiar. Or at least not one that I had felt for a very long time. I had no explanation for the reality of this sensation, nor did I try to generate an explanation, for that matter. Words didn't enter my mind. I was just present in the experience.

All I knew from that moment on was that I wanted not only to have that experience in my waking life but also to find a way always to experience that sense of inner presence wherever I was, no matter what the situation was. It was important for me to have it.

The quiet moment was a wakeup call. The complete absence of anger, fear, and mental noise made a stark contrast to everything I had been experiencing lately. I knew I had to become a new person and hoped I would find that person in a new environment that looked like the setting in my dream.

That same day, I went to work and filled out a vacation request form—but it wasn't a vacation that I was requesting. Vacations last a few weeks at best. This trip was going to be something more: a sabbatical.

I had all kinds of fears about taking so much time off. But my mind countered each fear that arose with a truth that restored my calm.

Fear: What if my manager doesn't approve my request?
Truth: Then, you find a new job.

Fear: What about money?
Truth: You have seven years of savings socked away in an equity fund.

Fear: What will happen to my clients?
Truth: I feel confident that I have their full support.

Fear: Is my vision clear enough?
Truth: Yes, it's clear. Remember the dream and how you felt elevated by it.

Fear: Where will I go?

Truth: The world is pretty big. You have options.

Later that day, I went online and spent a few hours researching places where I might stay across the globe, including Bali and Australia, and not finding quite what I was looking for. But I'll tell you. I had Costa Rica on my mind. I remembered my connection to that beautiful country and how much I had loved it. It was the place where I had faced my fear of heights by jumping off those two waterfalls. It was the place where I had let go completely.

And then, I found it, a needle in a haystack—a spot right on the beach in Costa Rica. I hadn't been told yet if I would be given the time off work, but it didn't matter. To go there just felt righter than anything I had ever felt, so I was willing to pay the price either way—with or without a job to return to. I went ahead and booked it. I knew my vision was to heal, to strengthen myself spiritually and mentally.

The prospect of my retreat overjoyed me. A few months alone in solitude, living on a beach, disconnecting myself from the external world—particularly social media, but also my cellphone—waking up early, meditating in the morning, and being in a state of creative flow would allow me to transform myself into a new man.

In the process of going back through the memories of my life, my stories, I was reminded of something about living in this expanding universe that emerged from a speck of nothing: Life is short, and change is inevitable. Before we know it, ten years can have gone by. No matter what, we get older. So, we should take care of ourselves. If we don't take care of ourselves, we may weaken or get sick. Some things in life could become harder as a result. We are not the same people we were ten years ago. But we are not the same people we were just last year either. The best we can hope for in the face of change is to adapt. To undergo evolution.

Because of the unavoidable certainty of change and the necessity of adapting to our circumstances, and because we are always facing challenges, we must develop internal skills and practice making good decisions and choices. If we think we have no options, it is because we decided to believe that this is true instead of looking for the limitless options that would be revealed to us if we opened our mental filters.

You can face challenges head on and develop strength and resilience. You can create a vision of the life you want. Or you can tell yourself what you may have been telling yourself your entire life that stopped you from trying. Whatever that limiting belief is for you which holds you back from having and doing what you want is your real challenge.

Time is the only thing you don't get back if you wait.

How each struggle changes you depends on you. But once you decide to accept the challenge, once you decide to go a certain way, you begin training your mind to support the choice. You must exercise your mind to increase its ability. To be ready. To stand your ground and be stronger when you would otherwise want to give up from weakness.

Accepting the challenge to evolve is not always comfortable. It won't necessarily feel good. You will feel like shit most days and try to find anything to make you feel good, so it is important that you start becoming self-aware. There's always going to be a voice inside you that says *It's too hard, it's impossible . . . and you're undeserving anyhow.*

This voice, which seems as if it would love to make every decision in your life for you without your full conscious participation, comes from your subconscious mind.

I'm no scientist, but my understanding is that the subconscious rules our lives. It's not a part of the brain, but more like a function of the whole nervous system and located throughout the body. The subconscious doesn't know the difference between a thought and reality, so no matter what you believe, it thinks it is true and real, which is a problem, if you happen to believe things that obstruct your progress, freedom, or happiness.

Everybody has beliefs buried deep inside them that dictate their thoughts and actions. In my experience, most people talk about wanting to improve themselves. But if they don't change their beliefs, then change isn't possible. The same old pictures in their heads and the same feelings will keep coming up. You can try to muscle your way through a change, like *Today, I'll start going to the gym in the morning,* or *I won't stay home another night and feel sorry for myself,* but one day you'll feel weak, and then the old behavior will be back, like a boomerang. The present can't let go of the past unless we examine our old, hidden ways of thinking.

For this reason, it's important to start writing shit down.

The way to recondition the subconscious mind is to write down your beliefs about whatever you think is limiting you and then replace them with new, better beliefs. For example, you might say: "I believe I am limited by my education, my age, and my financial situation."

To write in this manner, you have to switch into the mode of conscious thought. The conscious mind thinks logically and analytically, whereby the subconscious generalizes. We make most of the decisions in our lives based on generalizations, such as "I'm not smart enough," "I don't have enough experience," and "I'm not lovable."

The job of the subconscious mind is to uphold what the conscious mind believes is real. So, although the conscious mind controls less than 5 percent of our thoughts, if you analyze your beliefs and shift them rationally, the subconscious mind will fall in line.

If we don't start tracking the thoughts that are running through our minds, then we run the risk that the past will define us. Maybe you were six years old when you developed the belief *"Nobody cares what happens to me,"* and you've never updated it. By looking at it rationally, with your adult eyes, you can now see the truth that you've been receiving support right and left and dismissing its presence because you were focused intently on getting love and support from the one person you know who wouldn't provide it. With this insight, suddenly you are freed from thinking that has limited you for years. That's why we have to start looking at beliefs hidden in the shadows of our minds. That's why we must raise our consciousness if we're going to reprogram our minds to support us in creating the lives that we deserve.

As you know, I am an avid journal writer. The power of writing things down has been undeniably helpful to me in creating the life I want. The benefits are remarkable. That's why I am advocating this practice for you. Because of this practice, I began experiencing a major boost in my self-worth and confidence when I reviewed my journal. I saw areas of my life where I was allowing certain beliefs to hold me back from being happy, regardless of winning. Self-imposed limitations I had never looked at before. They were right there in my journal entries, as clear as day.

Through this exercise, I was able to get clear about what I wanted, and this gave me the confidence to start creating a more spontaneous way of life. Seeing my self-worth increase benefited me in every area of my life, including in the areas of my relationships and career path. This exercise also gave me a stronger purpose: to share my story and begin a path to helping other people. It led to me writing this book for you.

Here are a few things I believe you can achieve through regular journal writing. You can:

- Get into excellent physical shape.
- Move into a career that will bring you absolute joy.
- Meet the person you want to share your life with by tracking your actions.
- Heal yourself from painful memories by asking yourself the right questions.
- Take calculated risks by creating a detailed vision of what it feels like on the other side of the risk.
- Write a book by letting your imagination run free.

Three-Question Daily Journal Writing Process

The way to start focusing on what gives you energy in life, and living spontaneously in flow with that energy, is to write down your goal. This plants a seed in your imagination that you can nurture to grow.

The way is not to go on social media and pretend you have a happy life if you don't. And it's not to start living your dream life *fuckin' tomorrow.*

The way is to tell the truth to yourself and begin to change and have what you want, starting today.

Want to begin right now? Grab a pen and paper.

In the very beginning, when choosing what time of day is best to write, pick a time that suits your current habits, regardless of whether or not you want to change those habits. Further down the line, you may find, as I did, that journaling in the morning has great benefits. I do so to practice self-love and sustain deliberate personal growth. However, when you first start tracking your thoughts, you are going to experience change, which isn't always emotionally comfortable, so you need to go slow. It's best not to ruffle your feathers too much.

For example, if you're a night owl and used to sleeping in constantly, it won't get easier if you try waking up early to journal—not at first. Begin journaling in the evening, so you can genuinely commit to it.

This process is intended to help you decondition your mind and develop a more positive inner narrative. Your habits will begin to change as you build persistence and accountability with this one activity.

Every day, either morning or night, sit and write in a stream of consciousness for ten to twenty minutes. Engage your imagination in helping you build a vision of the life you want to lead and develop yourself personally to be the person living inside the vision.

The process is simple. Ask and answer three questions, writing about each in a stream of consciousness in any way you like (there are no rules or restrictions) for five minutes.

Question 1. Ask and answer: What would I like today to be like (or tomorrow, if you are writing at night) if it could be the best version of the day possible? More precisely, what would happen? How would I feel and behave?

Question 2. Ask and answer: What do I imagine could get in the way of me experiencing the ideal version of the day I've just described? Explore whether this is something true or something you made up and if shifting something inside you would help you stay in flow.

Question 3. If I could change what I think or how I feel today (or tomorrow) as the day unfolds, what would I change? More precisely, when I run into barriers to having the ideal version of my day—things interrupting my spontaneous flow, calm, and joy of being—how might I shift my behavior to keep the flow going? (Remember, we cannot control others, only ourselves.)

Put your journal away and do not read what you wrote until the weekend. At that time, look back over the events of the week and see if you learned anything or if something has shifted. By tracking and reviewing my journal every week, I was able to decipher several patterns that I wasn't aware of previously.

Once-a-Week Vision Exercise

Once a week, pick an item from your bucket list (see Chapter 8). Then, write about that item for twenty to thirty minutes, in a stream of consciousness. Write about how you feel about it, what you think is getting in the way of having this experience now, or soon, and what you could do to advance toward having it—or some variation of it—soon or even immediately. Write about who you imagine you'll be in that experience—meaning, what qualities of being you will embody.

There are no rules or restrictions. Come at the issue from different angles. See where it builds your energy. See if and where your energy feels drained. Notice how you can use your imagination to shift your energy and enthusiasm.

After you write for a while, pick one or two actions you could take in the coming week to advance the cause of actually doing this thing from your bucket list. In the next chapter, we'll discuss how this kind of goal setting can be integrated into your regular morning ritual.

Visioning is simple. You have to train your brain to know what you want. The brain doesn't have its own set of eyes. It lives in the darkness inside your head, and everything you see runs through your filters before your brain can begin to respond. Do this exercise so you can teach the brain to go after what you want, instead of allowing your old beliefs to make those ultimate decisions. The brain will take everything that matters into account, including how you respond emotionally to having this goal, what it does for your self-worth and confidence, and even how your physical body reacts to it.

After the revelation came to me in a dream that I needed to go to Costa Rica for a while and heal, and after I had booked my reservation for my trip, I began picturing what healing myself would look and feel like. This vision came from reviewing pieces of my past in the photo album of my brain, such as the stories I have been telling you throughout this book. I remembered spontaneously breaking down my emotional walls and discovering my vulnerability in Movement Class. I remembered when I gave my first live acting performance and forgot my lines, then found them again by spontaneously connecting intimately with my acting partner and the truth of the moment. I remembered standing above the most beautiful waterfall I had ever seen and spontaneously releasing my fear of death. Each of these experiences was a lesson or a test that shaped me.

ELEVEN

KNOW THE POTENTIAL OF YOUR MIND

Are you ready to grow?

Research concerning the flow state is incredible: Scientists are studying athletes who participate in action and adventure sports with incredible risks, like rock climbing and heli-skiing, people who can do incredible, next-level, superhuman things when their bodies are in a state of flow. Researcher Steven Kotler wrote an interesting book on athletes and flow, *The Rise of Superman.* In his research, he has found that the experience of all athletes when performing at a high level is similar. They fall into a mystical trance state as they confront possible danger.

As Danny Way, the first person ever to leap the Great Wall of China on a skateboard, puts it, "When I'm really pushing the edge and skating beyond my abilities, there's a zone I get into. It's the most peaceful state of mind I've ever known."[1] Their sense of time goes away.

Like other athletes experiencing flow, Danny's abilities increase when he's doing a difficult trick, and he is capable of making flawless decisions.

In a study of military snipers, Kotler found that their learning increased by 230 percent when they induced a flow state beforehand.[2]

When you are in a flow state, it has come about because you have completely lost yourself to one challenging task. Once you are immersed in it, there is absolutely nothing else you are thinking about. You're not thinking about yesterday's fight with your girlfriend or boyfriend. You're not thinking about your to-do list. You are 100 percent present, right there, right then, in the eternal now. That's flow.

Joy is associated with the flow state. There is a line we can follow from mindfulness to flow and joy. In groundbreaking research at the University of Chicago, psychologist Mihaly Csikszentmihalyi, Ph.D., studied *optimal experiences* and discovered that what made them genuinely satisfying was the state of consciousness we know today as flow. He coined the phrase. Through his research on the subject, seven conditions were identified that seem to be present when we are experiencing flow. He explains these conditions in a brilliant TED Talk he presented on the subject of flow back in 2004. In his words, this experience includes:

- *Complete involvement in what we are doing—focused, concentrated.*
- *A sense of ecstasy, of being outside everyday reality.*

- *Great inner clarity, knowing what needs to be done and how well we are doing.*
- *Knowing that an activity is doable—that our skills are adequate to the task.*
- *A sense of serenity, having no worries about oneself, and a feeling of growing beyond the boundaries of the ego.*
- *Timelessness—thoroughly focused on the present, hours seem to pass by in minutes.*
- *Intrinsic motivation—whatever produces the flow state becomes its own reward.*[3]

That is the potential of the human mind.

Flow is a universal human experience that does not belong exclusively to one group of people, notwithstanding that it is well-documented among creative artists and athletes. Mihaly Csikszentmihalyi says we can thank flow for the genius of Albert Einstein and how he described his state when he began hypothesizing his theory of relativity as that which is equal to the state of flow.[4]

Another example: It is well known how meticulously the actor Daniel Day-Lewis approaches every role, becoming so absorbed in flow as the character that even between takes, he remains in that state of flow.[5]

Surgeons apparently also can skillfully move through an eight-hour-long life-saving procedure with calmness and ease because they immerse themselves in this one incredibly difficult task. For them, time ceases to exist. They have each mastered this state. That is flow.

The Four-Stage Cycle of Flow

Flow is a state of being mindful, engaged, focused, and concentrated, feeling empowered, confident, loving, and worldly. It is the state in which we spontaneously serve our purpose, and nothing else matters as much. It is its own reward and makes us happy.

In Costa Rica, I devised a daily regimen to help me get into flow. I wanted the whole trip to be a process of self-love and growth. I wanted to program my brain so that flow would become my default mode in life. I was basing my regimen on Steven Kotler's investigations of elite athletes.

Although Kotler based his research on physical performance, the four-stage flow cycle he identified—struggle, release, flow, and recover—applies to every area of human endeavor.

- **Struggle.** Every flow cycle that is initiated begins with tackling a problem that currently seems unsolvable. To achieve flow, Kotler says, "We have to be willing to tackle challenges that are just beyond our current skill levels. We also need to amp up our focus and alertness."[6]
- **Release.** Release is letting go of the problem completely. A state of relaxation. In this state, according to Kotler, the brain is flooded with feel-good neurochemicals, like dopamine and endorphins, which are the body's response to stress and pain. The flow state itself comes only after the release state. The state of struggle will give way to the release state.

- **Flow.** When we're in flow, the region in the brain that acts as the inner critic, the *dorsolateral prefrontal cortex*, shuts off. Everything that Csikszentmihalyi discovered about optimal experience comes into play: clarity of mind, an ability to solve problems quickly, a heightened sense of well-being, and so on. There is a particular sense of stepping out of time that is extraordinarily pleasant.
- **Recovery.** As our effort comes to an end, our flow state ends. The brain and body enter a recovery phase in which it is possible (and likely necessary) to restore levels of neurochemicals, like dopamine. During this stage, we typically experience a mild "hangover" that inspires us to seek adequate sleep and engage in restful, downtime activities, such as meditation and reading.

Not only did I want to recreate that experience during my trip to Costa Rica, but I also wanted to engineer a life intention and devise a plan that would enable me to begin to live it every day of my life. The elevated emotional state from the dream was a catalyst for me. My desire to stand inside this scene changed the course of my life because it motivated me to shift from trying to control everything in my life to living more spontaneously.

In the month between the dream and the trip, I developed a master plan that led me almost effortlessly to have the experience I desired. It was my intention that made it possible.

The human brain can take everything you have known and fantasized about and create a master plan with it. What does this mean in pragmatic terms? For me, it meant I had said: "Hello, frontal lobe! Welcome to the show called my life and the unbelievable influence of my imagination."

The frontal lobe of the human brain comprises about 41 percent of the total mass of our cerebral cortex. This area is the workhorse of the brain, controlling almost every important cognitive skill we possess, from emotion, memory, attachment, and judgment to sexual behavior, creativity, and personality. When you add it all up, these factors form our reality.

The frontal lobe connects to every other part of the brain to create a blueprint for the life we are having. In essence, mine led me to the beach that early morning several months after my dream. But what really got me there was a question that I asked myself: "How do I retrain my subconscious mind to create a flow state?" That question drove me to find answers and rewire my brain "circuitry."

I understood that retraining my subconscious mind meant becoming someone new—with different neural connections in his brain than I had in mine. And I was willing and ready to commit to changing my personality to change my reality. I believed that if I practiced self-love, I could have the optimal human experience.

But how? I couldn't stand on a beach every day for twenty-four hours a day for the sixty days of my retreat waiting for my brain to solidify new neural pathways, right? That just seemed scientifically and humanly impossible. If I were to do this, I would need to get specific about the behavior patterns I repeated to stimulate the plasticity of my brain. I wanted a formula.

When we become specific, so do our physical conditions. From back in the day when I was bodybuilding, I knew this. I understood that if I could come up with a very clear vision of what a perfect day in Costa Rica would look like, then I could engineer the experience I wanted to have. And I wanted the engineering to encompass mind, body, and spirit. I understood the importance of empowering every aspect of myself. I was just as important to strengthen my mind as it was to keep my body strong and elevate my soul. This was the state of building flow.

The challenge of teaching every human being to live and create purpose in an elevated state of body, mind, and spirit is that we are conditioned creatures. We become the things we do. If we have been doing something else long enough, it is our default mode of being. If we are accustomed to being anxious, overwhelmed, frustrated, or angry, it will be easy to trigger those mental and emotional states in us.

But conditioning can work in our favor too if we do what is necessary to "rewire" our neural networks and permanently alter the default mode settings. That was what my regimen in Costa Rica was designed to help me do. The formula I produced to retrain my subconscious mind was to practice getting into flow. If all the studies I had read were correct, and I hoped they were, this would make it easier and easier to trigger a flow state in myself.

I wanted to test the theory that if I made the entire first two hours of every day my absolute favorite two hours of the day, I could accomplish anything I set out to do. I wanted to feel happy and in control of my destiny, like I was winning at life.

Why should these hours matter so much to you? Because these two hours are *your* hours, your time for solitude and reflection. They are all about loving yourself, loving the world, going through the process of healing (making yourself whole from anything that has had an adverse impact on you), and feeding yourself knowledge that relates to your chosen purpose before you give yourself over to other people's expectations and to honoring the commitments you've made, such as to your family, your employer, or your clients and customers. This is enough time in which to experience silence, repeat affirmations, set intentions, and define your own daily goals and accountability measures. By working on your mind with an open heart, before you start connecting with the outside world, you will ensure that you are available to do your best work.

My daily routine in Costa Rica was a ritual of deliberately expressing self-love for my mind, body, and soul. It went like this.

- *4:30 AM:* Waking up at the same time every morning and drinking a glass of water
- *4:35 AM:* Practicing meditation
- *5:15 AM:* Journaling (encompassing gratitude, goal setting, affirmations)

- 5:30 AM: Swimming in the ocean or another physical activity
- *6:00 AM:* Reading a book or watching a motivational video for one hour/make coffee
- *7:00 AM:* Start writing and find the state of flow
- *9:00 AM:* Quick break/fruit smoothie
- *9:30 AM:* More writing
- *Noon:* Lunch (more substantial, only fresh food, nothing processed)
- *1:00 PM*: Swimming in the ocean
- *2:00 PM:* Writing: Again, find a state of flow
- *5:00 PM:* Dinner (only fresh food, nothing processed)
- *5:30 PM:* Watching the sunset
- 6:00 PM *until bedtime:* Reading or viewing a video
- *Sleep eight hours every night*

In your life, knowing your own goals, you may wish to consider using the same exercise of reconditioning to start becoming the person you need to be to live the life you want for yourself.

Waking Up Early

I was surprised at how quickly I transitioned into the routine of waking early, given that since the bike accident getting out of bed had been my Achilles' heel. I credited the easy transition to two factors. First, the new environment. Second, my desire to be a better person and start kicking ass in the morning. Rising early would become the anchor of my days on retreat.

In Jon Kabat-Zinn's book on meditation *Wherever You Go, There You Are,* he writes:

> *The power of waking up early in the morning is so great that it can have a profound effect on a person's life, even without formal mindfulness practice. Just witnessing the dawn each day is a wake-up call in itself.*[7]

Imagine what it would be like to wake up early because all you can think about is your vision. What do you think it would do for your sense of motivation, your focus, and your self-control throughout the day if your vision for your best life were the first thought of your day? And if how you felt about this blueprint for your ideal life or favorite project—enthusiasm, gratitude, positive expectancy—was the first emotion that drove your thoughts and actions?

It would set a positive tone for your day.

The first two minutes of your day are the most important. This is when you unknowingly (or at least semiconsciously) decide what kind of day you're going to have.

It was my experience in the past that in those first 120 seconds my mind would quickly check in on all my memories of negative things that had happened the day before or the urgency, stress, and disappointment related to things I needed to get done. Right upon waking, I would start to feel anxious or depressed, which helped me decide that I would rather stay comfortable lying in bed for another hour or more than face the day. Those two minutes of anxiety would often stretch into another fourteen hours of trying to get comfortable with myself while I was going about my activities.

My decision to wake up at 4:30 AM every morning during the retreat changed my life. After the first two weeks of training myself to wake up before it was light, my internal clock started to wake me before my alarm. I woke up thinking about my self-love routine, feeling energized almost immediately. The way I ensured this was to roll onto my back, put my hands over my heart—keeping my eyes closed—and take ten long slow breaths all the way down into my belly while deliberately sending myself love. I played with different thoughts, like *Hello, Danny*, *I love you, Danny*, *Thank you*, *New day*, and even just *Love*. (Some phrases sync better with breathing.) And I made sure that the first two minutes every day were mirror copies.

The beauty of this gentle way of greeting myself lingered. I was more focused, more productive, and more able to exercise self-control throughout the day as a result of speaking affectionately to myself.

Setting a positive tone for the day was just the beginning of what I discovered from waking up at the same early time every morning.

Over time, the discipline and mental fortitude required to get up early will help you create a more organized mindset that spreads into every area of your life. Discipline will help you be more proactive; and as you take a more proactive stance in your life, your confidence and sense of personal agency to get things done will be heightened.

Meditation

My response to the results I witnessed from meditation, in a phrase: *You're telling me I had this superpower at my disposal all this time, and I didn't know it?!*

That phrase would have made me laugh up until the retreat, partly because the very idea of meditation had never really interested me, and partly because the few times I'd tried to work it into my life before, it was a far less than satisfactory experience. It seemed to increase, rather than reduce, my nervousness. Also, I'd been a gym guy my whole life, and the gym gang and meditation crowd never ran in the same social circles.

My first experience with the practice of mindful stillness, as you know, was in Movement Class at the William Esper Studio. Of course, I remembered the sense of vulnerability that came from being exposed to emptiness of thought, and how this released my body from stiffness. It also gave me the freedom to move without self-judgment. But other than the three times a week we met for class and spent ten minutes lying on the ground in Corpse pose, I hadn't practiced stillness.

What did meditation look like for me once I was living my vision? I started working seated meditation with a focus on my breathing into my morning regimen as soon as I booked my trip to Costa Rica, and it was almost laughable how quickly the chatter in my head switched on after I closed my eyes. Within seconds, I would be thinking about everything that was going on in my life—all at once. I tried shutting off those thoughts and focusing on my breathing, but that wouldn't last long. I'd begin wondering, *Am I breathing too fast? How much time has gone by?* And then I would get frustrated and quit.

After a week in Costa Rica, away from distractions and fully immersed in the process of my healing transformation, meditation went a little something like this: For about seven seconds, silence, and then, *Amazing! I'm not thinking. Is this meditating? It's so easy. . . . No wait, I'm thinking now. Damn it! How long has it been? How do people meditate?*

After a month in Costa Rica, the length of my meditation periods had gone up to anywhere between thirty minutes and an hour. One morning, I did a two-hour meditation because I was feeling overwhelmed from writing the day before.

Today, I engage in meditation almost as soon as I wake up every morning. I'll do a two-minute check-in, take care of my biological needs, then sit.

When I think about the man I was before I completely gave myself over to this practice, I don't even recognize him. It's been that profound of an influence in my life. So, what exactly changed that enabled me to be successful at meditation in the style I practice?

- **Concentration.** Meditation is a skill of attention. It teaches us to slow the thoughts running through our minds and realign ourselves with the natural flow of energy within us and around us, which greatly reduces our levels of stress hormones and propensity for anxiety, depression, and loneliness. An aspect of mindfulness meditation is concentration, the ability to focus on something specific for a sustained period. As Jon Kabat-Zinn says: "Concentration is a cornerstone of mindfulness practice. . . . You can think of concentration as the capacity of the mind to sustain unwavering attention on one object of observation. It is cultivated by attending to one thing, such as the breath, and just limiting one's focus to that."[8]

- **Breathing.** Meditation is a gift you give yourself and to the world. The power of that gift comes in the presence you bring to the moment. When you give yourself to each breath, you create an inner space that is timeless—which is why experienced practitioners can happily meditate for hours. An hour may only seem like ten minutes. Being present in this manner is profoundly healing. I'd never realized how shallow my breathing was until I started meditating, and it grew deeper and more even, and I became more present to it.

  Breathing is the deepest form of consciousness. By putting your attention fully on every breath that moves through your body, you begin to create a space between a stimulus and your thoughts. A thought cannot be present if you are fully aware of your breath moving through your body.

  If you don't believe me, try it and see for yourself what happens. Notice each breath moving air in and out, creating expansion in your chest and abdomen. If you notice your mind wandering off, then notice you are no longer present within each inhalation and bring your awareness back to your breath and the present moment. This is like an off-switch for your active mind.

As spiritual teacher Eckhart Tolle states in *A New Earth:* "You are not falling below thinking but rising above it."[9] By focusing on your breath and rising above thinking, you are creating a state of aliveness in yourself that most people will never experience.

- **Setting an intention.** In *Wherever You Go, There You Are,* Jon Kabat-Zinn writes: "It is virtually impossible, and senseless anyway, to commit yourself to a daily meditation practice without some view of why you are doing it, what its value might be in your life, a sense of why this might be *your* way and not just another tilting at imaginary windmills."[10] Bringing intention into your meditation practice is an incredible way to honor the practice for what it contributes to your life. There is a connection.

  Kabat-Zinn further states, "If you hope to bring meditation into your life in any kind of long-term, committed way, you will need a vision that is truly your own—one that is deep and tenacious and that lies close to the core of who you believe yourself to be, what you value in your life, and where you see yourself going."[11]
- **Mindfulness.** Once you are connected to the sensation of each breath moving in and out, with every release of air, you will feel as if you are dissolving into a sea of consciousness. This stillness creates the feeling that your body is floating in space. After every meditation

practice, I can feel my energy moving at another frequency. And I'm not quite able to think or feel. So why is this happening? By first setting an intention and then solely engaging in breathing after that, I open myself to receive. This is the point where meditation truly begins to develop our ability to concentrate.

There are many styles of meditation from which to choose. Here is the one I would suggest.

SIMPLE FIVE-MINUTE MEDITATION

Before you start practicing meditation, set an intention. Ask yourself what you want to accomplish today by meditating. For example, would you like to be grounded or peaceful throughout the day? Setting an intention opens the mind to receive.

Some people meditate in silence, and some meditate to music. The style of meditation you do is a matter of personal preference. You can find tons of calming music that is suitable for meditation for free on YouTube.

Pick a spot on the floor to seat yourself cross-legged or sit in a chair with a supportive back, sitting erect so your body can take in and release every breath fully. If you need to prop yourself up on a cushion to reduce stress on your hips and ankles, that's OK. It's important to be comfortable and at ease.

Start with the idea of breathing mindfully for five minutes. You can set a timer if you like or hold a watch in your lap that you can sneak a peek at without much effort.

Close your eyes. Then stay focused on the movement of the air that is your breath traveling into and out of the body. As long as you stay focused on your breath, your mind will remain calm.

The moment you become aware of inner dialogue give yourself right back to the practice of watching air. Leave the thoughts alone without worrying. Focus on the moment that is present to you, not the moments that have come and gone.

Notice how your body expands with each breath and creates more space. Once you find that space, you will start to experience an overall sensation of joy and gratitude.

Anytime you feel overwhelmed or burdened with self-doubt or stress, give yourself five minutes and see what happens. You might be surprised.

The current generation of children is being raised with cellphones in their hands practically from the moment they enter preschool. Similarly, we adults are exposed daily to computer screens, TVs, and the Net, and are never without our handheld mobile devices. We even sleep with them in our beds. Due to constant stimulation of our senses, we are constantly having our thoughts interrupted and redirected, in the process becoming less and less aware of what is happening in our immediate surroundings.

When our minds are wandering of their own accord, like this, we are usually experiencing a repetitive stream of information. You could experience this as thoughts about yourself, what other people think about you, and what's *not* happening in your life. More often than not, these thoughts have negative connotations, and their progression typically leads to unhappiness. Some people call this default mode the *monkey mind* because these thoughts are capricious and leap around like naughty monkeys in the trees, chattering at us. Meditation is the antidote to monkey-mind distractions, and more. You'll see.

After meditation, it's good to spend the next few minutes writing in a journal.

Daily Journal Writing

The emphasis I place on writing things down has to do with helping you specifically articulate what you want to see happening for you in the future. As I made abundantly clear in the last chapter, this practice will be instrumental in transforming and creating your life, regardless of the types of dreams you have—and furthermore, it will help you become the ideal you, the best version of the person you want to be.

As part of mastering your flow state, I emphasis journaling in the morning because it allows you with a fresh mind to begin your day by expressing gratitude for positive experiences of the day before, capturing the insights from your meditation, setting daily goals and intentions, and devising affirmations that will support you and serve your vision. You can trust yourself to decide what you want to write in your journal on the spot. Part of the art of spontaneity is flowing with what wants to happen or to be acknowledged.

Option #1. Express Gratitude

Making a list of things you feel grateful for is a beautiful way to start the day. This practice is especially helpful on days when you feel like you have *nothing* to be grateful for—because there is *always* so much to be grateful for if you take the time to look around. Expressing gratitude on paper permits you to accept the present moment as it is; it is in the little things we often overlook that you can find gratitude.

I'll give you three things right now that I bet you could be grateful for.

- *Your left arm.* Are you grateful for your left arm? Seems a little dumb to think about being grateful for a limb on your body that you've always had, right? I'll tell you someone who isn't grateful for having her left arm. Surfer Bethany Hamilton who survived a shark attack when she was thirteen and had her left arm completely bitten off.

  So, what else could she be grateful for? Her two beautiful kids and husband. Coming back a month after her attack and becoming one of the top female professional surfers on the circuit, winning many major competitions and inspiring millions of female athletes.[12] She has a lot to be grateful for . . . just not a left arm.

- *Your heart.* Are you grateful for your heart? I mean the one right inside your chest, pumping and feeding your body nutrient-rich blood. Are you grateful for your fully functioning heart? Let me tell you about a good friend of mine, Josiah Gonzales, who can't be grateful for a fully functioning heart. Josiah was born with aortic stenosis, which means his aortic valve is too small, so the blood flow through it seals off, and his heart has to work harder to pump blood into his body. When he was four years old, during a cardiac catheter procedure, young Josiah went into cardiac arrest, and his heart stopped for forty-five minutes while his medical team kept pumping blood into him to keep his brain alive.

  What could Josiah be grateful for? Everything else he has accomplished. He says, "Living a normal life, with a massive physicality hindering you, trying to navigate how half my heart has to work harder than everyone else's is a challenge. It makes every other challenge not seem so hard, even pretty damn easy."[13] Josiah can be grateful for being alive—I get it. Cool. But he can't be grateful for having a fully functional heart like most of the rest of us can.
- *Your mind.* Are you grateful for your memories? I watched my grandfather live the last three years of his life with full-blown dementia. He didn't remember a thing. He wasn't able to ask or answer questions, and I'm not quite sure he knew who I was anymore. We take our memories for granted because, of course,

memory is not something we think about as being fragile until we get older. Sometimes we use this capacity as a mechanism to cause ourselves to suffer, instead of a source of lessons or a treasure chest for beautiful experiences. But once your mind is gone, you're not you. You lose your history and with it your personality. You become a prisoner of time.

For what could my grandfather have been grateful at the end? I doubt he even knew.

If you only focus on what you don't have or not having it yet, then you're not going to be an energetic match for the thing you want because gratitude is an energetic currency. Combining a vision with gratitude is an extremely powerful setup for building into your power because you are creating energy by finding gratitude for elements of your life that align with your vision. This allows you to set up daily goals and create affirmations to support that vision.

There's always something to be grateful for. It doesn't have to be complicated. Release your expectations of how you think this needs to look and give yourself over to the feeling that works for you at the moment.

Option #2. Record Your Daily Goals and Small "Wins"

It takes time to attain or manifest big life goals. It is the sum of every little goal that you achieve that creates a pathway in your mind which helps you actualize your dreams. In recording your daily goals on paper, you open your mental filters so you can spot opportunities. This is just what I did when I was looking for a place to travel and found the article on Costa Rica.

Nothing is of greater importance to achieving goals and realizing a vision for your life than measuring your progress. Every day is a new platform to learn more from your failures, your insights, and tracking the small, seemingly insignificant progress that is bringing you closer to your larger objective. By tracking small wins, including even the ones you might consider too small, you are building a positive, confident mindset.

How to start tracking your daily goals and daily progress? Think of a goal, such as showing yourself more love throughout the day. Then write down a handful of ideas about what you specifically could do today to show yourself more love.

Option #3. Create Daily Affirmations

You may recall how, as a youth, I used affirmations to support myself in adhering to my eating plan while training as a bodybuilder. Phrases such as "I am strong," "I am intentional," "I am reaching for my dreams today" can help us to align with our goals and approach life with calm certainty. Ultimately, we are what we focus on.

Words are powerful tools to direct our focus. They can rapidly shift our mindset in a new direction. It also helps when we believe what we are saying or thinking.

After practicing gratitude and setting daily goals, ask yourself how you want to be defined. Do you want to be strong? Do you want to be lovable? Do you want to have more confidence? Then, tell yourself *I am strong, I am lovable. I have more confidence.* Better yet, write it down. Don't make it complicated—just a few words, priming your brain for flow.

You can purchase a blank book in which to write either online or in almost every bookstore. Start at the top of a new page each morning. Jot down motivational quotes, insights, observations—whatever you like.

Physical Activity

Fitness has been a big part of my world for almost half my existence, yet only in the last year or two have I started to realize how far the effects of exercise go beyond the body. The brain is profoundly affected by movement.

The key to movement's positive impact on cognition is *brain-derived neurotrophic factor* (BDNF), a protein present in the hippocampus, an area of the brain related to memory, learning, and stress control. With morning exercise, you can lower your cortisol levels and keep them low for the entire waking day. In his book *Spark*, psychiatrist John J. Ratey, M.D., reports that more than 5,400 studies of BDNF have been done. In one, "researchers found that if they sprinkled BDNF onto neurons in a petri dish, the cells automatically sprouted new branches, producing the same structural growth required for learning."[14]

Ratey calls BDNF "Miracle-Gro for the brain."[15]

In a 2013 study in *The Journal of Sports Science and Medicine*, it was found that twenty to forty minutes of aerobic exercise increases BDNF in the bloodstream by 32 percent.[16] The reason exercise is a key trigger for learning is that it improves the function and growth of neurons; in doing so, it fosters linkages between thoughts, emotions, and movement.

When engineering your daily routine, I advocate doing your physical activity in the morning. In my experience as a personal trainer, there are many benefits associated with the habit of waking up and going to the gym early in the morning. The people who do tend to be highly focused and well-organized go-getters who have deliberately formed habits that maximize their productivity. They recognize that more movement means more brain activity and clarity.

Being off the grid in a tropical paradise for a few months posed an interesting challenge for me: no free weights or weight machines. Since I could remember, I hadn't gone longer than a week without strength training. Lifting weights was part of my daily routine back home. And I loved this routine. I never had to talk myself into going for a workout. Going to the gym in the morning was as automatic as brushing my teeth.

No gym in Costa Rica? No problem. I knew I wanted to include movement in my morning regimen after meditation and journaling. At 5:30 AM, right around the time the sun was rising, I swam in the beautiful warm ocean water for twenty minutes. Due to the high concentration of minerals in the ocean water, including magnesium, calcium, and sodium, the effects on my skin were incredibly healing. I also found that being weightless in water in a natural environment and forming a stronger, more regular breathing pattern while swimming was calming. These things stimulated my parasympathetic nervous system—promoting the *relaxation response.*

I customarily followed up my swim with a series of bodyweight movements designed to boost my muscular endurance, which included max-rep pushups, squats, and controlled sit-ups. *Max rep* just means, do it until you can't do it anymore. Though I would not be lifting the heavy weights that I was used to at the beach, I determined that I could still train with physical intensity as part of my journey of self-mastery.

I highly encourage you to schedule thirty minutes of fitness activity into your daily routine. Walk briskly or jog around the neighborhood before work. Bike. Swim. Lift weights. Also, take notice of what happens with your level of focus, concentration, ability to do daily tasks with clarity, sleep quality, self-esteem, and confidence in the next few weeks and then journal about these results. Establishing a new exercise regimen is always hardest at the beginning, but once you notice the changes in your life and see how much energy you have and how much better your mind functions, then you'll feel enthusiastic about your decision to get started. Your impulse to move your body will become automatic if you persist.

At the beach, I followed my physical workout either by reading for an hour or going right into my writing work—in which case, I would read later in the day or before bed.

Reading and the Pursuit of Knowledge

Once you have opened your mind, fill it with tons and tons of wisdom.

Where do I begin? You can choose to chill and watch Netflix and tomorrow ask your coworkers if they saw *Sex Education* . . . Or you can read *The Alchemist* by Paulo Coelho and get a deep insight into your own life. Maybe you'll start thinking about crafting your legend, as his lead character did.

You can choose to spend the next hour flipping through Instagram, and make sure to like at least fifty reels to get maybe (at most) half the number of likes back . . . Or you can fall asleep at the end of a long day reading *Tools of Titans* by Tim Ferriss and use the great insights from millionaires and billionaires that Ferriss gathered. Investing in your life by adopting some of their little techniques could pay off with massive dividends later on.

You can choose to get high and eat a massive bag of caramel-covered Chicago Mix Popcorn off the floor while picking it up because you ripped open the bag too hard, then wake up the next day, a few hours after sunrise, feeling like you just got hit with an unreal hangover (stag parties excluded) . . . Or you could decide to learn from and be inspired by reading the biographies of some of the greatest historical figures ever to have lived, individuals like Sir Winston Churchill, whose courage in rallying Great Britain and the Allies to fight Hitler and the Axis forces instead of surrendering to them helped to end World War II. Isn't it interesting that he was able to do so much although he suffered from depression?

Or read about Albert Einstein, not just because of his incredibly high IQ, but because his brilliant imagination changed what we know about how the universe works. He gave his entire life to his work.

Or read one of the many books about Nelson Mandela. Take your pick. Learn about a man of conscience who lived by such a set of strong values, among them focus, will, and determination, that despite living for almost thirty years as a political prisoner inside prison walls, when released he wasn't angry, he wasn't bitter, and he united his country as its respected leader, which was his dream. Read what he said when he was awarded the Noble Prize.

And men aren't the only ones who do cool things. Read about the social reformer Susan B. Anthony, a Quaker who at age seventeen circulated a petition to end slavery in the United States and then played a pivotal role in women getting the right to vote—although she died fourteen years before she could see the fruits of her labor. We could learn a thing or two about social activism and justice from a committed individual like Anthony.

Or read a biography of bestselling author and media darling Julia Child who in the 1950s defied our expectations not only of women's abilities in the kitchen and life but our expectations of what we are capable of as we age. She was the first female chef to receive le Grand Diplôme from the renowned Parisian culinary academy the Cordon Bleu, an accomplishment she achieved at age forty. Then she went on to write the bestselling cookbook of all time, *The Art of French Cooking*, and host an Emmy Award-winning television show (the first of several cooking shows) starting at age sixty.

Knowledge is the precursor to experience. You can choose to do the same things you've been doing your entire life and not understand why nothing new is happening for you, or you can start to explore all the possibilities. Wondrous things could happen to you. Reading puts answers in your hand devised by people who have solved every problem you could have. There are no new problems.

You can learn from others' mistakes and triumphs. With a few exceptions, everything that can happen to us has happened to somebody somewhere sometime and been recorded in a book. Reading helps us prepare to have what we want.

I'll give you two examples of what reading could do for you.

First, let's say you feel your body and mind are wearing down, and you're diagnosed with some illness that could become fatal. You need to change, but you don't know how. You don't know where to start. A good friend of mine, Liana Werner-Gray, wrote *The Earth Diet*, a book about the lifestyle and approach to nutrition that saved her from going down a deep hole after she was diagnosed with a stage one tumor. Through her book, Liana has helped hundreds of people face similar health challenges. Before Liana, Kris Carr wrote *Crazy Sexy Cancer* about how she changed her life and survived stage four cancer. Amazingly, both women started to write *before* they recovered. *During* their struggles to find a new way to be.

Second, let's say you feel stuck or a little lost and you're fighting daily battles with your thoughts. Maybe there's something you want to achieve in life, but you can't seem to make any traction on it, or you're miserable because you're in debt, or maybe you're successful and affluent, yet still you're not happy, and you don't know why. Books on how to change our inner experience can be transformational.

Let me tell you about one such book that changed my life, *The Monk Who Sold His Ferrari* by leadership expert Robin Sharma. I had this book in my possession for a few years, intending to read it until I forgot I had it. I found it in a box while cleaning my apartment and decided to read it that coming Sunday, which I did entirely in one sitting. If you haven't read this book, I highly recommended you do. It's a fable.

Sharma's story goes like this. A successful lawyer with every "toy" imaginable, including a Ferrari and private plane, has a heart attack in court and realizes he has to make a change. He's had enough stress, anxiety, frustration, and anger. Then and there, he spontaneously decides to quit his law firm, sell all his possessions, and move to India without telling anybody where he's going. He comes back many, many years later, looking thirty years younger and surprises his former apprentice, now a lawyer himself, in his office late one night. This once-upon-a-time lawyer, who came near death and basically was reborn, tells his apprentice of his journey of living with monks, the purpose of life, and ten rituals of radiant living.

Incidentally, I read this book when I started thinking about what needed to change in my life. Everything I read in the book was at the back of my mind. One quote stuck with me.

> *There is no chaos in this Universe. There is a purpose for everything that has ever happened to you, and everything that will happen to you. . . . Every experience offers lessons. So stop majoring in minor things. Enjoy your life.*[17]

I carefully selected twenty books to bring with me on the trip to Costa Rica, which included Sharma's and other personal favorites. (See Recommended Reading.) The first book I read at the beach was *The Alchemist* by Paulo Coelho, about a boy named Santiago seeking his purpose, who finds himself going through all sorts of so-called setbacks and lessons and has "random" encounters with people, which turn out to be not so random. After reading about Santiago, I retraced my steps to arrive where I was in my mind, thinking about all my life-shifting encounters. I challenge anyone to read this book and not see how his or her own life is like a puzzle of experiences that fit together.

Reading books changes our lives.

If you make reading a daily habit, for example, by setting aside an hour a day to read, the way you look at life will immediately start morphing. By building a habit of reading every day for a minimum amount of time, you will begin to see ways to improve many areas of your life. You will stimulate your mind and improve your mental acuity. You will expand your creativity. You will exercise your powers of focus and concentration. You will develop more empathy. And you will learn to express yourself with a deeper sense of truth and tranquility.

Motivational Videos and Documentaries

Motivational videos, such as TED Talks, and podcasts are incredible educational tools. In Costa Rica, I watched a documentary every other night, featuring characters like Albert Einstein, Nicola Tesla, and Alexander the Great, and subjects like World War II and quantum physics. Studying how great minds think and how the world has changed in the last hundred years is another way to expand your knowledge and appreciation for human innovation. It wasn't until I had watched a documentary on World War II that I fully realized what a blessing it was to be born with everything we have in our day and age.

I recommend watching interviews, conference panels, and speeches delivered by today's greatest motivational speakers. My favorite speakers on these videos and podcasts included people like Jay Shetty, Tony Robbins, Eric Thomas, Gary Vaynerchuk, Tim Ferriss, Brené Brown, Mel Robbins, Joe Dispenza, Tom Bilyeu, Joe Rogan, Evan Carmichael, Marie Forleo, Robin Sharma, and Oprah Winfrey, of course.

Watch videos that inspire you. Make specific choices to view videos on subjects you want to learn. There is so much information out there, offered freely by amazing experts and people who have gone through experiences you may be going through. If you don't like reading, watching videos is more important. Start by watching for thirty minutes a day.

Eat Food That's Nourishing for Your Mind and Body

Part of knowing the potential of your mind is fueling your body with the right food and being conscious of how it makes you feel. Fuel for the body is fuel for the mind, and if the mind and body are not polluted and are connecting, beautiful things start happening.

To be clear: I'm not going to offer you any restrictions or rules for how to eat in this section of the chapter. I'm only going to describe what I did while I was in Costa Rica and how it impacted me. You are the expert on your own body. And so much information is available on what to eat to live your healthiest life that any contribution from me would be overkill. There are so many experts to advise you.

And there is no single answer. Eating right comes down to one thing: We are all different, our bodies are different, and as Charles Darwin's findings on evolution will tell us, we are what we ultimately adapt to by way of environment.

The only thing I intend to comment on is mindfulness while eating. I'm just going to talk about the practice of *conscious eating.*

There is no way around it. What we put in our bodies matters. But I want to tell you that it might not be for the reason you think. We all know that food directly affects the body, and if the food is poor quality, then it will do bad things to the body. What has only been brought up recently, through research and studies, is that food has a direct and intimate connection with the mind.

I remember the first time I learned about the connection between body and mind.

Microbiologist and neuroscientist Ruairi Robertson, Ph.D., gave a brilliant TEDx Talk entitled "Food for Thought: How Your Belly Controls Your Brain." He begins by explaining that it has been proven that our intestines are physically linked to our brain through the vagus nerve, which sends signals in both directions.[18] However, he then says:

> *Interestingly, even if this* [the vagus nerve] *is severed, our intestines can still continue to function fully without a connection to the brain, suggesting they have a mind of their own. Secondly, our brains are made up of a hundred billion neurons, which continuously send messages to tell our bodies how to work and behave. Well, interestingly, our GI tracts (guts) have a hundred million neurons. Thirdly, our microbiomes are the center point of our immune systems; meaning, a disturbance down here (in the gut) can cause subtle immune reactions all around the body, which, if prolonged, can affect brain health.*[19]

In other words, when our food is unprocessed, our entire nature is unprocessed—pure and natural. The quality of our minds depends upon the quality of the food with which we feed our bodies. If the food isn't pure, let's say because it's filled with saturated fat, chemicals, or sugar, the mind doesn't settle down after eating. It will constantly be jumping from thought to thought, or we will become drowsy and mentally sluggish.

As Robertson says, "Our health is so dependent not only upon nourishing ourselves, but upon feeding other living microorganisms inside of us."[20]

Food is an adjunct to exercise and meditation. If you eat carefully, it can help you develop a stronger mind and body. If you're interested in mastering your inner life (which means mastering your thoughts and behavior), then it matters how you fuel your body, mind, and spirit. As you're learning what you need to include in your formula for self-mastery, aim to be conscious of how you respond to the food you eat. Journal about it so you can measure these effects on you and your lifestyle over time in terms of energy, clarity, and mood.

In Costa Rica, I chose not to eat any meat and took my protein from eggs and lentils. Everything grown there was organic, and they had the best selection of fruits and vegetables I'd ever seen, so I would pile my shopping cart high with avocados, cucumbers, tomatoes, celery, watermelons, bananas, blueberries, strawberries, mangoes, papayas, coffee, and spices such as turmeric, cinnamon, basil, cumin, and ginger whenever I went to the grocery store. In essence, I was selecting a wide range of nutrient-rich brain food loaded with vitamins, minerals, antioxidants, and many anti-inflammatory and stress-relieving agents.

Remember, my goal in Costa Rica was to retrain my subconscious mind so that the flow state would become its default mode setting.

Every morning, right after I woke up, I drank a glass of water. But I wouldn't have anything solid to eat until 11 AM—after completing my morning regimen of activities—because digestion draws energy away from the brain and the muscles. I practiced the dietary strategy known as *intermittent fasting*. This is where you take in nothing between the hours of 8 PM and 8 AM. It's a twelve-hour fast at a bare minimum. You can extend it to sixteen hours.

I prefer to meditate and to exercise on an empty stomach, and I love the healing effects the body goes through when it hasn't eaten for some time.

I have heard mixed things about whether or not drinking a cup of coffee is considered "breaking the fast." I chose to drink coffee after having my initial glass of water. Then, at 11 AM, I would start my food consumption for the day with a fruit smoothie.

Lunch usually came around 1 PM. This would be a massive salad with lots of different colors of veggies, four eggs, lentils, avocado, and olive oil. I wouldn't eat again until 4 PM. I ate watermelon at night.

After the first week of this schedule, I found a significant difference in the feeling I had in my gut. It was as if I had received a massive lift. I believe that I soothed some inflammation. I had fewer hunger pangs. I was able to focus more on reading and writing because I was thinking less about what I was going to eat next. And I became much more aware of how my body and mind reacted to eating my meals.

After the first month, the overall calming effect of the food, the ocean water, and being outdoors so much of the day was very healing for my body and spirit. The lifestyle I was pursuing had taken years off my body and face. The effects the food had on my mind were equally beneficial. My mind could stay calm. My thoughts did not jump around. This could have come from a properly running digestive system that was not sucking out all my energy to work overtime. I was more focused on what I was trying to accomplish.

There is an intimate connection between the food we eat and our emotions. I will say, at times of deep reflection and life-changing self-discovery, our food should always be unprocessed and nontoxic. Flow is a byproduct of a healthy mind and body.

Challenge: Seven Days to Induce Flow

I challenge you to try the same morning routine I did in Costa Rica for seven days if you feel like it's time for a massive shift in your life. If you decide that you won't do it, I'm guessing it's because you know or suspect that you *can't*. Let that sink in.

Here's how it's going to work. For seven days, while otherwise going about your life as it is, wake up two hours earlier. Use these hours to:

- Meditate.
- Write in your journal, expressing gratitude and recording small daily goals you set.

- Develop an exercise or movement routine.
- Read books on subjects that most interest you.
- Work on a task that nourishes your goals and vision. For example, you could practice playing guitar, learning Italian, or shooting photos for an exhibit you want to put up in six months. This task has to be challenging enough to induce flow. It helps to add a sense of urgency through creating a deadline and working backward from that in stages.

It's helpful to decide how and when you want to fuel your mind and body and stick to a plan. Putting aside a few hours a day like this will help you to get into a flow state, and possibly maintain it throughout the day. The specificity of the goal by a certain date helps you to measure your progress.

If you have a family, you can do a shorter practice each day, and do it at whatever time of day is possible for you. Find an hour and twenty minutes for your routine.

Devote the first twenty minutes to meditation, with the intention to align with your soul and create a vision for your ideal life. To get in a state of flow with bringing this vision to fruition write about it in your journal, paint or draw images of it, read supportive literature, or just keep meditating. Make sure you do find time to read, engage in fitness training, and eat consciously to keep your mind strong.

Track everything for seven days and check in with any dialog going on inside of your head—notice what's uncomfortable and investigate the reason why. What's the fear?

Keep asking yourself questions instead of giving up. Journal everything you are thinking—don't hold back.

If you can get to seven days, keep going. Start reading more and more books to expand your mind and allow that vision that's steadfast in your heart to start working its way into your body and your thoughts.

Now, if you try this for seven days and you can't do it . . . Or if you can't or won't commit to waking up early . . . Or if you felt that you had to watch television or you had to eat that bag of Doritos after the fourth night . . . Or you felt a crazy level of anxiety or you're feeling depressed and nothing is helping despite trying to get up two hours earlier, then I present you with an alternative.

Super Challenge: Go Off the Grid for One Month

If you want to go deeper, take off one month from work, as I did, and book yourself a little cabana on the beach somewhere off the grid far away from civilization. I highly recommend Costa Rica because of its breathtaking sunsets, and quiet beaches, where I practiced self-mastery and wrote my first draft of the manuscript for this book. By changing your environment and routines and taking on this completely scary challenge, you are committing to a journey of self-love and discovering your true potential.

Find out who you genuinely are. You don't know who you are. Chances are that the way you see yourself is the way you think everybody sees you. But that's not who you are at the core. Only you can ever know how everything works inside your heart, your mind, and your soul.

Take a month, disappear, dance naked on the beach, plan to read at least ten books, and discover your heart space, the exceeding power of your mind, and the state of flow. Become like a ninja master in whatever it is that you sometimes think about mastering when nobody is looking. Spend one month in paradise, if you can't handle the seven-day challenge in your usual environment.

TWELVE

TRUST YOURSELF IN THE WATER

Can you give yourself to the process of your life?

I could not have picked a better destination than Costa Rica to heal, retrain my subconscious, and cultivate the wonderful state of flow. The country had the most incredible skies to explore, breathtaking sunrises, glorious sunsets that inspired me every night to go out and watch them, and magnificent ocean breaks that I felt profoundly blessed to be swimming in. I couldn't have asked for anything more. I was closing a chapter in my life and starting a new one, created from an internal strength of will and purpose. The trip was preparation for a life that promised to be every bit as spontaneous as it would be fulfilling.

I can pinpoint the exact moment at which the page turned for me. The moment was easily the most terrifying of my life, as well as the most beautiful. I had never experienced an intersection of two powerful states of being before, like that.

It was during the final week of my trip. I hadn't seen another human being for a few days, and I'd started to think I was the last person alive on the planet. I had a very introspective feeling.

This particular early morning started like every other morning of my retreat.

I woke up early, as usual. I first had a glass of water and practiced my meditation before finding my way to the water, and as was my custom, I planned to come back to my cabana after my swim and spend the hour writing down all the things for which I was grateful.

However, there was something very different about this particular morning.

I first noticed it when I opened my front door and saw how strong the winds were—more bluster than usual. I could see from the top of my balcony that the waves of the ocean were heavier than normal. The skies were darkening above the beautiful Pacific Ocean.

It was a breathtaking sight.

What can this be? Hurricane? Tropical storm? A very heavy tropical storm?

I wasn't expecting a sunrise that morning. That was clear enough. No matter. All I could think about after my meditation practice was that first dip in that beautiful water, maybe catch the last swim before we got hit with heavy showers. I made my way to the waters as I did at the same time every morning, and I walked over to the same spot as I did every morning. After nearly a month getting to know this paradise, I could say I knew the area well. It was covered by a large rock formation on the ground, about seven feet beneath the surface of the water, which was always clear, to walk over midday when the waters were calming. I picked this spot every morning because of the formation of waves.

I loved swimming against the waves. From all my rituals in the morning, swimming in the ocean was up there as my favorite. It was a workout for the body and mind, and it was a hell of a lot of fun. I sat momentarily at the crest where the water seemed to get pulled back into the ocean. I always enjoyed time reflecting on the beach before my swim.

I had never seen skies quite so ferocious and yet, there was this very calming effect, at the same time. It was chaotic and it was peaceful. It was stunning to witness two extremes, unwavering, meeting at a cross point.

The waves were far from small. I remember thinking about how perfect these waves would be to surf. I had no surfboard, but I was taking in the beauty of the entire experience before I would make my way into the waters.

I was particularly thinking about jumping into those larger than usual, beautiful waves. I checked for a spot where I could enter safely. I saw a clear path forward, between a series of massive waves coming on shore. I stood up and let the water wash over my feet, taking small steps forward between the extreme force of the water being pulled back in. I kept walking through the rock formation until I was waist deep. I felt a pull from the water getting a tiny bit stronger as I got further in. I looked at the shoreline behind me, which was about ten feet from where I was standing. Then I looked forward and saw a clean spot ahead, an opening in the ocean that I could dive into and make my way toward some big, beautiful waves.

Once I dove in, headfirst, I noticed how forceful the movement of the water was that morning. I was being pulled out to sea. I looked behind me and noticed that I wasn't ten feet from shore anymore, but more like twenty. *How did that happen?* I thought.

I went underneath again, and when my head came up this time it was clear that I had been taken a few feet more. Noticing how far I was being pulled into the ocean, I started fighting against the ocean's hold on me. At that point, I realized that a rip tide had captured me.

Suddenly, I felt it. I felt death crawl inside me. I felt it try to take me. I felt death punch me right through my chest and start squeezing all the oxygen out from my heart. Panicking, I felt sure there was no way I was going to survive this. The ocean was too powerful. This was how I was going to die.

I was barely holding onto the seabed with my two big toes. I kid you not. I was using them to tightly grip the jagged edges of the ocean's floor. My eyes were barely over the lip of water. From my point of view now, the sandy shores looked like a thin line wavering above the churning water.

I was about to be sucked out into the ocean, and no one would even know for days that I was gone; and by then, I would be floating shark food, miles away from civilization.

Everything happened so fast. I didn't have time to think about solutions. I wasn't thinking anything. My inner narrative was KOed. I was operating 100 percent on intuition, vulnerability, faith, and the absolute certainty that I wanted to live more than anything.

My first reaction was to swim forward against the current. But the more I tried to fight it, the further I could feel myself getting pulled in. I knew time was against me. I had to decide what to do in the next few seconds. Because I was in between heavy waves heading toward shore, I knew my only chance of surviving was to get to those waves.

I took one single massive breath and held it. I let the water pull me down and grabbed onto the rocky ocean floor with both hands, getting a secure grip against the rock formation on the seabed. Then I started propelling myself slightly forward, leveraging the resistance of the water and pulling sideways, trying to use the power of the waves going in the opposite direction to save myself.

At that moment, I drew upon all my will and called out to every single cell in my body to give me strength. Things are not the same underwater. Gravity does not exist. I had no clue if I was making any progress toward shore. I didn't know how much gas I had left in me. I just knew I couldn't let go. And I had no idea which direction I was going or where I would find myself when I came up.

I had no other choice than to trust that I was guiding myself in the right direction.

I felt my grip weaken finally. I needed air. I let go of the bottom. As I made my way to the surface to take a breath, a massive wave slammed right into me. At this point, all I could do was pray.

Once I found my head above water yet again, I looked up and saw the shore in view. Another wave hit me faster than I could clear my eyes. And in an incredibly powerful rush of water, it dragged me back to the sandy beach.

When I realized I wasn't going to die anymore, I could feel how hard my heart was pounding. I felt a few fresh, jagged scrapes running down my back which came from the wave slamming my body against the ground like a rag doll.

Panting, I felt how much oxygen I had consumed. I can't point to any measurable source, but if I had been wearing diving gear, I would tell you it was the entire tank—because that's how it felt. Every muscle in my body had been activated at once and was now completely exhausted.

I could even feel my soul dragging its feet from exhaustion. I could barely walk back to solid ground. With the water still knee-high, I dropped to my hands and knees, gasping more and more, and crawled until the water was only skimming my toes.

That's where I stopped, gasping for every ounce of air that had been taken out of me. I clenched my hands into a fist and plunged them deep into the sand, so relieved that I could.

My body was shaking uncontrollably.

My gasping for air suddenly turned into a downpour of tears falling from my cheeks onto the ground. I have no idea what came over me, but I couldn't hold anything back. I didn't know what triggered the sobbing—whether it came from believing I was going to die or from how happy I was that I didn't. But I couldn't stop.

Between the tears and heavy gasps for air, I remember releasing a loud yell. I didn't give a fuck about anyone hearing me. I yelled so loudly that I heard stray dogs begin barking and running closer toward me. And I yelled out again. And then again and again.

And then, from my hands and knees, I let go of holding myself up and rolled onto my back with my feet flat on the wet sand and the palms of my hands resting beside me. The water was still skimming my body. I let out another loud shout.

What emotion was I feeling?

It was everything, all at once, happening at the same time. I could still feel death so close to my heart, but I could feel life even closer. I had a feeling of acceptance. Of everything. It was terrifying, and it was beautiful: life and death at an intersection.

Suddenly, without any explanation, thought, or design, something shifted inside me, and my intense tears turned into tears of pure joy. I started laughing with complete abandon. In that beautiful moment, logic out the window, I was the last living person in the world. It was this unreal, absolute I-don't-give-a-fuck kind of joy that I have never, ever felt so palpably. And still, I cried. I took deep inhalations while releasing, accepting, and allowing.

Every sensation was as vibrant as I have ever felt—even the rough wetness of the licking from the dog that surprised me with a tongue bath on my face, which I had summoned by yelling at the top of my lungs. Everything in that moment was a complete joy.

I sat up and looked straight ahead. The storm grew stronger and was coming closer to shore. It was an unbelievable sight. About half a mile out, there were dark clouds formed into a traveling funnel. I couldn't look away. Like a sign from up above, the formation broke free and began spinning across the water. I couldn't believe what I was witnessing—and right after barely escaping death, no less. A massive waterspout was lasering through the ocean.

I couldn't look away. I couldn't run away. Mesmerized, I stayed and watched it for as long as it stood and grew, never coming close enough to shore that I felt I needed to get away and seek shelter. Eventually, it came apart, as all things do.

Soon after, the beach was hit with a massive tropical storm, unlike anything I'd ever seen before—with winds going as high as seventy miles per hour, trees being rocked hard against each other, violently swinging back and forth.

Back under my roof, I was writing about everything that was going through my heart and mind. The sound of the heavy rain was so strong that it pierced the walls of the cabana. I thought about that small fraction of a moment in the ocean when death almost had me, only one tiny instant among millions and millions. But remarkably heightened.

To this day, the feeling of it is still with me. In my heart. A sinking feeling. The next moment was when all the life lessons I've been describing to you came together. That was the moment when all the internal strengths in me coalesced; and the glue that held them together was the trust I had in myself.

When there was no other option, when it came down to sink or swim, I trusted myself. I trusted my instincts.

I could have died and I was so grateful to be given another chance at life. Nothing else mattered. Not the bullshit I left back home. Not the fears. I wrote in my journal how grateful I was for that near-death experience—if I can accurately call it that. Not because I survived, but because it happened.

There are no mistakes. There are lessons. Everything is downloaded in you.

A chapter in my life ended that day.

A page turned.

A new chapter began writing itself.

For a long time, I believed happiness was predicated on success, and that success was determined by how many friends you had, how much money you made, and how many countries you traveled to. Each time I ticked off a box on this list, I felt more secure. I thought I was "winning" at life, but my definition of winning was incomplete.

The external circumstances of my world were strong, and my internal narrative was "I am winning," but in fact, I was allowing my environment to dictate my moods and thoughts.

That morning, as I was regrouping from being pulled away from shore by a riptide, I was at complete peace with myself. The source was internal. I wanted to be internally driven.

The word *spontaneous* means "without reacting to an external stimulus." To live spontaneously means you are unforced. Uninhibited. Free.

A spontaneous life is not defined by the big moments we experience. It is made through a process of small, everyday moments that add up to the sum of our success and happiness. To let go and live spontaneously is not easy. Although it's simple, it's also hard work. It's a process.

If you want to experience the benefits of spontaneity, you have got to work at it. You have got to know you want to get to the level in life where you can do anything that gives you absolute passion. But you have to trust the process, and you have to trust yourself.

You have to trust yourself in the waters of your life.

You have to trust that every current in the ocean is there for a reason. Trust that every pain and struggle is given to you to make you stronger. To teach you a lesson. To help you discover your true character. To help you know yourself better. To sharpen what's in your mind and your heart.

To be happy and feel fulfilled, you will need to believe you are strong enough to break through the obstacles to your goals. To earn your results, you may have gone through significant pain; you may even have bled or suffered for what you achieved. After you have failed and stood back up, fell down and stood up, again and again, you will know that you are stronger than you have ever been.

And then something else happens—beyond your results.

One day you wake up, and you find yourself seeing the world differently. Your heart feels full. Your thoughts and soul are aligned. You have a clear vision of what you want. You come to peace with everything in your life, including your past, where you are now, and where you see yourself going. And nobody will ever be able to take this feeling of wholeness and clarity away from you.

On the other side of each struggle you surmount, you will feel an overall sense of peace and joy. This is something that cannot be created by any external stimulus or circumstance.

The only way I know to get there is to trust yourself and know that your life is directly in your own hands. When you know this, you can find the power to transform, you can find purpose through connection, success through focus, and action through accountability. And this is what the world wants and needs from you.

You are going to have to go internal and start learning how to reengineer your subconscious mind, trusting your intuition, breaking your walls down, keeping faith in your heart by looking for how every moment is a gift and opportunity. You will have to learn the power of visualization and creating life through your struggles. You are going to have to trust the process. And once you begin to take away all the layers, one by one, and you uncover your joy, you can cultivate it through setting, and then adhering to, a standard you want to live by, by developing rituals that uphold it.

Next time you walk into the ocean—any ocean, whether literal or metaphoric—remember, the struggle you feel is within, no matter what wave overtakes you. Trust yourself in the waters.

ACKNOWLEDGMENTS

When I think about how my manuscript came to be, I think about a lot of people that were part of this journey. I think about the people that never gave up on me when I was writing this book, and those I knew before this book was even a real thought in my mind who've always shown me love and will always be a part of my life journey.

I would like first to show love and gratitude to **my mom.** I know raising me on your own wasn't easy. You did great with everything you knew. Thank you for the karate lessons and always making me homemade steak sandwiches. Mostly, thank you for always encouraging me to go after my dreams.

Next, a special thanks to my amazing editor, **Stephanie Gunning.** You helped me through many tough times to make my dream a reality. Working with you on my manuscript will forever be remembered as a masterclass for me in becoming the writer I needed to become and will continue to be, and that to me is a priceless gift. Thank you, Stephanie.

Thank you, to **my grandmother,** for all those French tutorials and talks we had about books and great writing.

Miguel Boccanegra. Nobody believed in me more than you. For six years, you told me every day to "finish my book." When others gave up on me, you stood with me. I will never forget that.

Chris Retsinas, One of my best friends from high school. We trained together through our first bodybuilding show. We went to Cancun together. I got through hard times with you, and I have so many incredible memories that you were a part of. You never forget my birthday.

Rachel Bausch. We have memories together in three cities, New York City, Los Angeles, and Vancouver. But the best memories will always be New York. You will always be my family and I will always be yours.

Jorge Valdes. We met through a catering company in New York. We started training together. We became best friends. We became brothers. I started my fitness career because you insisted I get my personal training certification.

Vanessa Barg. You continue to inspire me by demonstrating the trueness of courage and strength. There was a time you hired me. You believed in me. You will always be in my heart.

Liz Rosa. There are not many people I can say this about, but I could not imagine I would be where I am right now in my writing career if not for knowing you and working with you. You did not just elevate me as a writer, you've been an incredible friend and you've always had my back. And I will always have yours.

Mehdi Mehrtash. First, you were my client. Then we became very good friends. You have given me your time and expertise to help me build a website I love. You always go above and beyond for the people in your life. I will never forget your generosity and loyalty.

A special thank you goes to my fantastic acting teacher of two years, the late **William Esper** and the staff of the **William Esper Studio**. It was a tremendous honor to study the art of acting with Bill, not to mention, a few of my favorite teachers, Nancy Mayans, Deb Epstein Jackel and Per Brahe, And to my Esper Family, the classmates with whom I spent two years breaking down my emotional walls: Lucia Evans, Nicholas Blue, Mary Boies, Brianna Barnes, Juan Luis Acevedo, Michael Steinbrick, Susan Dalton, Will Blagrove, Reg Lewis, Chris Triana, Josiah Early, and Lindsay Nader, and anyone I forgot.

A few more people I want to make sure I send love: Gabriel Kava, Giles Panton, Norm Despins, Caleb Bomysoad, Jeremy Reinbolt, Andy Abbani, Holly Anderson, Patrick Warburton, Rick Sparrow RIP, Judah Ratzlaff, Daniel Purgal, Georgia Victoria Fletcher, Jonathan Ben David, Laurent Beique, Ramsey Nached, Bobby Skafidas, Elisha Buckley, Annastasija Koch, Seth Devlin, Michael Lyons, Rita and Sony in Costa Rica, Alana Drozduke, DJ Tre Funk, Erica Minisini, Laurent Beique, Michael Lyons, Michael Cárrasco, Simran Jagpal, Chris Murdoch, Nicole Whittle, Parsa Pourjafar, Danica Lin, Andrew Abraham Alcalde, Ray Martin, Nastasia Liavas Genova, Martha Kendall, Solomon Chin, Vince Rocco, Juvel Jeo Jose, Avery Spavor, Daniel Watson, Phil Malpass, Runie Malpass, Amara Kraft, Mandy King, Daniela Dib, Nicolas Mezger, Leija Turunen, Lisa Paris, Luciana Faulhaber, Carrie Villar and Alex Zachariah.

Gus Yoo. Thank you for taking the time to create a cover I absolutely love. It is everything I envisioned. You captured the essence of my book perfectly. I look forward to working with you on many more book covers.

NOTES

ONE: WE HAVE THE POWER TO TRANSFORM OURSELVES

1 *Scarface*, screenplay by Oliver Stone, directed by Brian De Palma (1983).

2 *Pumping Iron*, screenplay by Charles Gaines and George Butler, directed by George Butler and Robert Fiore (1977).

SIX: A MASTER CLASS IN VULNERABILITY

1 George Sylvester Viereck, "What Life Means to Einstein," Saturday Evening Post Society, Indianapolis, IN. (October 26, 1926).

2 William Esper. From my class notebooks.

3 William Esper and Damon DiMarco. *The Actor's Art and Craft: William Esper Teaches the Meisner Technique* (New York: Anchor, 2008), p. 39.

4 Ibid., pp. 39–40.

5 Bréne Brown. *Daring Greatly: How the Courage to Be Vulnerable Transforms the Way We Live, Love, Parent, and Lead* (New York: Avery, 2012), p. 9.

6 Loch Kelly. *Shift into Freedom: The Science and Practice of Openhearted Awareness* (Boulder, CO.: Sounds True, 2015), p. 194.

7 Brown, p. 45.

8 Esper and DiMarco, p.114.

EIGHT: MY GOALS MADE ME DO IT

1 Christopher Taibbi. "Brain Basics, Part One: The Power of Visualization," PsychologyToday.com (November 4, 2012).

2 John Rampton. "Neuroscience Tells Us How to Hack Our Brains for Success," Entrepreneur.com (June 16, 2017).

ELEVEN: KNOW THE POTENTIAL OF YOUR MIND

1 Steven Kotler. *The Rise of Superman: Decoding the Science of Ultimate Human Performance* (Houghton Mifflin Harcourt, 2014), pp. 5–6.

2 Ibid., p. 87.

3 Mihaly Csikszentmihalyi. "Flow: The Secret to Happiness," TED.com (February 2004).

4 Ibid.

5 Matt Trueman. "Did Daniel Day-Lewis See His Father's Ghost as Hamlet? That Is the Question," TheGuardian.com (October 29, 2012).

6 Kotler, pp. 118–22.

7 Jon Kabat-Zinn. *Wherever You Go There You Are: Mindfulness Meditation in Everyday Life* (New York: Hyperion, 1994), p. 180.

8 Ibid., p. 72.

[9] Eckhart Tolle. *A New Earth: Awakening to Your Life's Purpose.* (New York: Penguin, 2008), p. 246.

[10] Ibid., p. 75.

[11] Ibid., p. 76.

[12] Victor Mather. "Bethany Hamilton, a Shark-Attack Survivor, Reaches an Unlikely Crest," *New York Times* (May 31, 2016).

[13] Private conversation with Josiah Gonzales.

[14] John J. Ratey with Eric Hagerman. *Spark: The Revolutionary New Science of Exercise and the Brain* (New York: Little, Brown and Company, 2008), p. 40.

[15] Ibid., p. 19.

[16] Matthey T Schmolesky, David L. Webb, and Rodney A Hansen. "The Effects of Aerobic Exercise Intensity and Duration on Levels of Brain Derived Neurotrophic Factor in Healthy Men, "*Journal of Sports Science and Medicine*, vol. 12, no. 3 (September 1, 2013), pp. 502–11.

[17] Robin Sharma. *The Monk Who Sold His Ferrari: A Fable about Fulfilling Your Dreams and Reaching Your Destiny* (New York: HarperCollins, 1998), p. 90.

[18] Ruairi Robertson. "Food for Thought: How Your Belly Controls Your Brain," TEDx Talks Channel/YouTube.com (December 7, 2015).

[19] Ibid.

[20] Ibid.

RECOMMENDED READING

These thirty books, organized alphabetically by title, have strongly influenced my thinking on spontaneous living.

The 5AM Club: Own Your Morning. Elevate Your Life by Robin Sharma (New York: HarperCollins, 2018).

The 10X Rule: The Only Difference Between Success and Failure by Grant Cardone (Hoboken, N.J.: Wiley, 2011).

The Alchemist by Paulo Coelho (New York: HarperCollins, 1993).

Atomic Habits: An Easy and Proven Way to Build Good Habits and Break Bad Ones by James Clear (New York: Avery, 2018).

Awaken the Giant Within: How to Take Immediate Control of Your Mental, Emotional, Physical and Financial Destiny! by Tony Robbins (New York: Simon and Schuster, 1991).

Becoming Supernatural: How Common People Are Doing the Uncommon by Joe Dispenza (Carlsbad, CA.: Hay House, 2019).

Can't Hurt Me: Master Your Mind and Defy the Odds by David Goggins (Austin, TX.: Lioncrest Publishing, 2018).

Crushing It!: How Great Entrepreneurs Build Their Business and Influence—and How You Can, Too by Gary Vaynerchuk (New York: HarperBusiness, 2018).

Einstein: His Life and Universe by Walter Isaacson (New York: Simon and Schuster, 2008).

Flow: The Psychology of Optimal Experience by Mihaly Csikszentmihalyi (New York: HarperCollins, 1990).

The Gifts of Imperfection: Tenth Anniversary Edition by Brené Brown (Center City, MN.: Hazelden, 2020).

Limitless: Upgrade Your Brain, Learn Anything Faster and Unlock Your Exceptional Life by Jim Kwik (Carlsbad, CA.: Hay House, 2020).

Long Walk to Freedom: The Autobiography of Nelson Mandela by Nelson Mandela (New York: Little, Brown and Company, 1994).

Man's Search for Meaning by Viktor E. Frankl (Boston, MA.: Beacon Press, 1959).

Mastery by Robert Greene (New York: Viking, 2012).

Meditations: Adapted for the Contemporary Reader by Marcus Aurelius, translated by James Harris (2016).

Mindset: The New Psychology of Success by Carol S. Dweck (New York: Random House, 2006).

A New Earth: Awakening to Your Life's Purpose by Eckhart Tolle (New York: Penguin Life, 2005).

Outliers: The Story of Success by Malcolm Gladwell (New York: Little, Brown and Company, 2008).

Relentless: From Good to Great to Unstoppable by Tim S. Grover with Shari Lesser Wenk (New York: Scribner, 2014).

Sapiens: A Brief History of Humankind by Yuval Noah Harari (New York: HarperCollins, 2015).

Spontaneous Healing: How to Discover and Enhance Your Body's Natural Ability to Maintain and Heal Itself by Andrew Weil (New York: Knopf, 1995).

Start with Why: How Great Leaders Inspire Everyone to Take Action by Simon Sinek (New York: Portfolio, 2009).

Straight Shooter: A Memoir of Second Chances and First Takes by Stephen A. Smith (New York: Gallery Books, 2023).

The Power of One More: The Ultimate Guide to Happiness and Success by Ed Mylett (Hoboken, N.J.: Wiley, 2022).

The School of Greatness: A Real-World Guide to Living Bigger, Loving Deeper, and Leaving a Legacy by Lewis Howes (Emmaus, PA.: Rodale Books, 2015).

Think Like a Monk: Train Your Mind for Peace and Purpose Every Day by Jay Shetty (New York: Simon and Schuster, 2020).

Thinking, Fast and Slow by Daniel Kahneman (New York: Farrar, Straus and Giroux, 2013).

The Untethered Soul: The Journey Beyond Yourself by Michael A. Singer (Oakland, CA.: New Harbinger, 2007).

Wherever You Go, There You Are: Mindfulness Meditation in Everyday Life by Jon Kabat-Zinn (New York: Hyperion, 1994).

RESOURCES

DANNY DAVID WEBSITE

https://dannymindbody.com

INSTAGRAM.com/dannymindbody

TIKTOK.com/@dannymindbody

FACEBOOK.com/danny.david

LINKEDIN.com/in/danny-david-a9b77a192

YOUTUBE.com/RawFitnessGuy

ABOUT THE AUTHOR

Danny David is an elite personal trainer and biohacker who writes about mindset, fitness, and the flow state. He lives in Vancouver, Canada.